On May 27, 1977, Margaret and Pierre Trudeau announced to a shocked world that they were beginning a ninety-day trial separation.

Immediately there ensued a barrage of questions: What had changed the loveable, gorgeous young woman whom the Prime Minister had married into a free-wheeling, unconventional jet-setter? What will happen to the children? What will Margaret do with her new life?

Answers to these questions are revealed for the first time in this unauthorized biography of Margaret Trudeau, by Arthur Johnson. You will find here not only what changed Margaret while she lived at 24 Sussex, but also some up-until-now secret tales of her life before her marriage.

——Read for the first time about Margaret's mysterious seven-month trip to Morocco. . . .

——Find out what the priest who married the famous couple thought of Margaret. . . .

——Get an inside view of life at 24 Sussex—including reports from the servants who lived with the Prime Minister's wife for six years. . . .

——Learn about Margaret's views on life, love, marriage, sex, freedom and most importantly—why she had to leave her life in Ottawa to pursue freedom in another country. . . .

MARGARET TRUDEAU

by Arthur Johnson

PaperJacks LTD.

Markham, Ontario, Canada

AN ORIGINAL CANADIAN

PaperJacks

One of a series of Canadian books
first published by PaperJacks Ltd.

MARGARET TRUDEAU

PaperJacks edition published November, 1977

Cover design by Brant Cowie

Black and white photographs by Rod C. MacIvor,
United Press International
Color photograph by Rod C. MacIvor

Ben Wicks' cartoons courtesy of Toronto Sun Syndicate
With thanks to researcher Britt MacLeod-Nichols

ISBN 0-7701-0059-7

Contents

1
The Beginning: Introduction

In the beginning, it was the love affair of the century, the storybook romance, the marriage made in heaven. Hollywood couldn't have topped it, this union of multimillionaire playboy Prime Minister and luminescently beautiful flowerchild bride. The love affair was all the more compelling because it was true. Not only was it true, but at the time it seemed appropriate, almost necessary, a work of Nature rather than a contrivance of man. Coming when it did, after the turbulent sixties when the generations were split asunder and contemporary society divided into the "over-thirties" and the "under-thirties", the "May-September marriage" of Pierre Elliott Trudeau and Margaret Joan Sinclair seemed an inspiration to heal the wounds, to reconcile the differences, to usher in the 1970s in peace, love and harmony.

From a distance, it seemed idyllic: the Prime

Minister's good-humored jests about married life; Margaret's stunning smile, her perfectly formed teeth and bubbly high-spirits; bouncing baby boys born on Christmas days. And it was, for awhile. As marriages go, the early years of the Trudeau union were better than most. To be certain they had their obstacles to overcome, the age difference between the fifty-one-year-old Prime Minister and his twenty-two-year-old bride being chief among them. It was said, too, that they were opposite personalities: he, a cold, distant intellectual, she, a warm, spontaneous, almost naïve woman for whom the emotions were paramount. But it seemed that their differences were complementary, that this marriage of opposites would make Pierre Trudeau more human and his bride less flighty.

For the public, the timing of their marriage was auspicious. Jacqueline Kennedy had long since cast aside her widow's demeanour to marry into the secluded, sybaritic life of Aristotle Onassis, the Greek shipping billionaire. The public, amazed at the outrageous excesses of her million-dollar shopping sprees, had turned away from America's former first lady; she had lost the appeal of her tragic splendour.

Margaret, on the other hand, all sweetness and simplicity, seemed like the first dewy rose of a summer morning pushing aside the stale lilies. She exuded good health and good breeding. In appearance, she was as wholesome as the oatmeal cookies her mother used to bake back in the Sinclairs' rambling house in West Vancouver, and as a bride she retained that little-girl quality, enormous blue eyes that leaped like frisky colts during animated conversation. Her flawless complexion suggested an adolescence untouched by trauma; the vitality of her attractive figure attesting to years of skiing and swimming at the world's most fashionable resorts. There was a madonna-like lustre to her finely drawn features, and in person she was even more beautiful than her photographs.

But the passage of six years wrought a subtle, terrible change. Something was drastically wrong in the Trudeau marriage and by its end, Margaret had undergone a drastic transformation. It could be seen in her face: gone was the open, trusting, vulnerable quality that had instinctively drawn people to her. To be sure, she was still, at twenty-eight, a beautiful woman, but she had hardened. Somewhere in the middle of her marriage, life for Margaret had become a battlefield, in her words, "a bloody revolution of the mind". The struggle and the defeats had made her fine features into a taut, grim mask.

At the end of May, 1977, after months of scandal, rumor and speculation about Margaret's odd behavior, the true depths of the tragedy became known. The world's most famous marriage was over. Margaret's escapades, most notably her "ultimate freedom trip" to Toronto visiting with the notorious Rolling Stones and her lengthy visit to New York where she launched a controversial photography career, had kept her name in the headlines. The world had waited, fascinated, for each new installment of what had become almost a television soap opera. A terse statement from the Prime Minister's Office was the final episode in the marriage of Margaret Trudeau:

May 27, 1977

Pierre and Margaret Trudeau announce that because of Margaret's wishes they shall begin living separate and apart.

Margaret relinquishes all privileges as the wife of the Prime Minister and wishes to leave the marriage and pursue an independent career.

Pierre will have custody of their three sons, giving Margaret generous access to them.

Pierre accepts Margaret's decision with regret and both pray that their separation will lead to a better relationship between themselves.

As this announcement flashed onto millions of television screens across North America, viewers must have asked themselves one question: WHY?

Why would a young woman, blessed with a husband who was kind, attentive, wealthy and famous, a woman with three healthy children, with, in short, almost everything she needed to lead a happy life, throw it all away for a dubious career in a cutthroat business? How could Margaret, devoted as she was to her children, choose to leave them in their crucial formative years to live the life of a swinging singles photographer in the streets of Manhattan?

There is no simple cut-and-dried answer, it would seem. Rather it is more likely a combination of personality traits dating from childhood, and of trying circumstances which Margaret could never have foreseen when she had so determinedly set about as a girl barely out of her teens to win the Prime Minister as a partner in marriage. Her flight from the restrictions of marriage, motherhood and official life in Ottawa was a foregone conclusion some say, quite in keeping with her little-known fling in Morocco before she took up seriously with the Prime Minister. But more about Morocco later. . . .

For many people, the public life of Margaret Trudeau is a fascinating series of question marks sandwiched among bizarre public utterances, flamboyant demonstrations of complete disregard for protocol or public opinion, gossip, rumor and the fading image of a stunning young woman helping unwittingly to dispel that stolid gray image of Canada. A conspiracy of silence among friends, relatives and other people close to Margaret has until now made much of her life a shadowy, vague thing. The silence is remarkable, in itself. Later, the reasons for this secrecy will be examined.

One question has persisted since the Trudeaus' secret wedding ceremony in Vancouver: how did a young woman who, except for her beauty, had no apparent signs of distinction, manage to catch the Prime Minister? Dozens of other equally beautiful women had tried, but until he encountered Margaret, Pierre Trudeau appeared destined to remain Canada's most eligible bachelor. Was it, as the Prime Minister has claimed, her beautiful blue eyes? How did she overcome his conviction that a marriage between two such opposite people was doomed? How did she win over her parents, who were opposed to their daughter marrying a man old enough to be her father? Was it more than chance that brought Margaret and the Prime Minister together again in Vancouver after a brief flirtation on a tropical island two years earlier? Some of the answers to these questions will emerge later as the Trudeaus' clandestine courtship is revealed.

Margaret once said that the Prime Minister had taught her "a lot about loving", and she rarely referred to the other men in her life before her marriage. Thus, few people knew about her romances at Simon Fraser University in Vancouver, the hotbed of student dissent on Canada's west coast. What did she learn from the radical young Englishman who was suspended from his teaching job in a political dispute with the administration? Why were her parents opposed to Margaret going steady with this man? What happened during her affair in Morocco with an Arab, a man much older than herself? We will see how the early love affairs in Margaret's life profoundly influenced her character as a mature woman.

The turning point in Margaret's life was the highly publicized nervous breakdown she suffered in 1974, midway through her marriage. Her confinement in a Montreal hospital was mysterious. It came with no advance warning that the Prime Minister's young wife was anything but normal and well adjusted. Adding to this mystery was the coverup attempt by the Prime Minister's Office, an attempt that backfired when Margaret herself told the world she was under psychiatric treatment for emotional problems. We will see that Margaret had her own reasons for desiring to escape from a life that had become almost intolerable.

For most of the six years of her marriage, Margaret was confined to the stifling atmosphere of the Prime Minister's official residence in Ottawa. The free spirit who had flitted about the exotic regions of North Africa and the ski slopes of British Columbia came to value freedom above everything else in her life. She also grew to fear the repressive effects that armed policemen and a fleet of servants were having on her children. In several interviews, Margaret hinted about the escapes she had attempted, the secret journeys she had made to preserve her sanity. Disgruntled servants have also whispered about Margaret's curious behavior as chatelaine of the huge old mansion which she shared in Ottawa with the Prime Minister. (One of their odd tales involves meditating to please the whims of their mistress.) The truth about Margaret's fears of violence at 24 Sussex Drive will also be revealed later in the book.

As a beautiful woman with subtle charm and a powerful husband, Margaret was the recipient of lavish gifts and hospitality. Her charm and her husband's influence gave her access to some of the world's most famous, wealthy and most talented personalities. From a privileged but obscure upbringing in Vancouver she was thrust into the center of political power in Canada. The clash in lifestyles—from west-coast hippie, complete with flowers and bluejeans, to a member of the international jet-set almost overnight— entailed a traumatic adjustment.

One may try, as Margaret did, to preserve the simplicity, to take the good and ignore the rest. But inevitably the narcotic attraction of being a celebrity, the dazzle of famous people and beautiful things surfaces. Offered on a silver platter, the chance of becoming Margaret Trudeau, Superstar, was too strong for her to resist.

It was a terrible temptation to place before any woman of Margaret's age and temperament. On the one hand she had the somewhat dull and tedious existence of a housewife and mother. On the other lay the dazzling prospect of a brilliant career as a photographer of beautiful people and fascinating places.

Without knowing all of the forces at work on Margaret, it would be easy to condemn her out of hand. But to understand her it is necessary to get behind the hard, cynical mask she has assumed since the start of the long chain of events that led to the shocking, spectacular breakdown of her marriage. In order to understand Margaret as she is today, one must begin at the beginning.

'Aside from your role as a
happy Canadian Prime Minister's
wife, have you ever done any
other acting?'

2

The Childhood of Margaret Trudeau

When Margaret Joan Sinclair was born in Vancouver on September 10, 1948, she entered a world of quiet, middle-class affluence. It was a warm, hazy fall day in the large city nestled between the Pacific Ocean and the Rocky Mountains on Canada's west coast. Eagerly awaiting her arrival home from the hospital were three sisters—Heather, six, Janet, three, and Rosalind, barely a year old. If her father, James Sinclair, a rising young politician, was disappointed that his latest offspring was not a son, he did not show it. He'd become almost resigned to ruling over a household of women. Margaret's mother, Kathleen, a handsome woman who devoted herself to being a good wife and a conscientious, loving mother, was just as happy to have another daughter.

Vancouver in 1948 was a sedate, scenic city, perhaps a bit provincial, but beginning to bustle in the first flush of prosperity following the end of the Second World War. The men who had gone off to fight had had three years to settle back into the routine of civilian life and resume their careers, and, almost as if obeying some law of Nature, raising children to replace the soldiers who had fallen on the battlefield. Jimmy Sinclair was one of the men who had returned from the fighting; Margaret was one of the hundreds of thousands of children born during an era that sociologists later called the post-war baby boom. The hospital nurseries were crowded and doctors found themselves answering more and more middle-of-the-night telephone calls that sent them rushing off into darkness to fetch new life, red and squalling, into the world. Gradually it built into something like a floodtide. New hospitals were built, and the push was on to train or import more doctors. To meet the pressure of all these new families, new subdivisions in the city sprang up. Vancouver, like most other cities in Canada and the United States, was being transformed.

And what of all the post-war babies? They were being brought up by a formula which went roughly like this: good nutrition plus good education plus good manners equals, ultimately, the good life. It translated: eat your vegetables, study hard and don't talk back and you'll get a good job (or a good husband) and will always be happy.

When Margaret was born, Jimmy Sinclair had been a Member of Parliament for eight years. He was brilliant, charming, hard-working, and stubborn. This last trait, stubbornness, proved a stumbling block in his early political career; he passed it on to Margaret, and in some measure, to the rest of his daughters as well. As a young Liberal M.P., he was often too quick to show his dislike for the Prime Minister, William Lyon Mackenzie King. It was almost inevitable that Jimmy Sinclair would not see eye-to-eye with Mackenzie King, one of Canadian history's truly great eccentrics. But it was impolitic. Mackenzie King was a spiritualist who never held an election without first consulting a medium; a prime minister who never forgot a slight. Mackenzie King informed Sinclair in no uncertain terms that he would never advance in politics as long as he was Prime Minister. And he didn't.

When he was first elected to Parliament in 1940, Jimmy Sinclair wore the uniform of the Royal Canadian Air Force. He was soon sent overseas, and acquitted himself well as a squadron leader in the desert air force during the North-African campaign. His wife, Kathleen, and Heather, the baby, were left in Vancouver to share a house with Kathleen's sister, whose husband was also in the services. When he was discharged in 1945, Sinclair resumed his place in Parliament, biding his time until Mackenzie King was succeeded as Prime Minister by Louis St. Laurent. Under the new Prime Minister, the political fortunes of the Member of Parliament for Capilano rose quickly.

In 1949, Sinclair's diligence and dedication in

the House of Commons was recognized by St. Laurent, who promoted him to the position of Parliamentary Assistant to the Minister of Finance. It was a sure sign that he was on his way up the political ladder. But it also meant a great increase in his responsibilities. Almost a year to the day after Margaret's birth, he moved his family from Vancouver to Ottawa.

It might seem at first then, that Margaret absorbed politics with her pablum, but it wasn't so. Although Kathleen Sinclair was extremely proud of her husband and his political career, a man's work was a man's work and his home was a place for family activities, not political debates. The beginning of the 1950s was also a much quieter era in Canadian politics than the one that had preceded it. If one was determined enough about it, the affairs of Parliament need not be tracked into the home.

With the family established in Ottawa, Jimmy Sinclair continued his ascendency: an apprenticeship as assistant to the Minister of Trade and Commerce in 1951; and in 1952, a plum: his own portfolio. He was named Fisheries Minister.

But throughout it all, the Sinclair children remained almost untouched by politics. Occasionally, they were brought to the House of Commons to hear their father speak. But they were never dragged along on election campaigns and their mother continued to keep aloof from the affairs and intrigues of Government. Jimmy Sinclair, however, was digging himself in deeply. By 1957, the talk around Ottawa was that he might run against Lester Pearson for the leadership of the Liberal Party. The prospect did not please Kathleen Sinclair. With a large house to run in the posh Rockcliffe Park area of Ottawa and five daughters to look after (Betsy had been born in 1951) she had her hands full. Serving as a Cabinet Minister was occupying more and more of her husband's time and it was not promoting harmony in the home.

Margaret was doing well in public school by this time, a pretty little nine-year-old with dark, curly hair and an appealing manner. With her parents and sisters, there were occasional flashes of temper. But Jimmy Sinclair and his wife stood for little nonsense and she never really threatened to become a discipline problem. However, growing up in a family of girls—and all of them bright and attractive—was a constant struggle for attention and Margaret began to develop her own distinctive, outgoing personality.

At the age of ten, Margaret's life changed abruptly. In fact, life for all of the Sinclairs was disrupted. The winds of change had swept across Canada. A thundering orator from the prairies of Saskatchewan, John Diefenbaker, had led the Conservative Party into power, scattering the forces of the long-reigning Liberals. Fifty-year-old James Sinclair was one of the casualties. After eighteen years in politics, he suffered a humiliating personal defeat, and his career in Ottawa was over. With five young children to support, he was forced to seek a job outside Government. Fortunately, his political connections stood him in good stead and he was soon hired as head of the Fisheries Association of British Columbia. The family moved back permanently to Vancouver.

All things considered, Jimmy Sinclair's unhappy exit from politics turned out well for daughter Margaret. She had done so well in school in Ottawa that when she started in at a Vancouver school, the principal immediately pushed her ahead one grade. That meant she was a year younger than all of her classmates. But with little effort, she was soon at the top of her class again. Moreover, she made friends easily. Her teacher, too, took an immediate liking to her. Because Margaret was so much smaller than the other children in the class, and also because she was so eager to please, she was made something of a teacher's pet. In Grade Five, that wasn't a bad thing to be. She was chosen to run messages around the school and given other little marks of special status.

As it turned out, being defeated in politics was hardly a disaster for Jimmy Sinclair. Soon he was earning a much more substantial amount of money than he had as Fisheries Minister. The family moved into a pleasant home in the exclusive Capilano Highlands area of North Vancouver. In a few years he became a top executive for a cement company and purchased an even more imposing home down the street. He had come a long way from the struggling Depression days when, despite his engineering degree and studies at Oxford on a Rhodes scholarship, he'd been forced to take a job teaching school. But Jimmy Sinclair had perhaps been born lucky. Even his teaching job had had its rewards: one of them being his wife.

Kathleen Barnard, the daughter of a prosperous Vancouver businessman, had been one of his students—the top mathematics pupil in his class.

Despite the fact that Jimmy Sinclair was fifteen years her senior, student and teacher had felt an immediate mutual attraction. They were married in 1940, when she was a student nurse and he a fledgling Member of Parliament. Was it just coincidence that Kathleen's daughter, Margaret, grew up to marry the Prime Minister, a man twenty-nine years her senior? Perhaps it was. But Kathleen Sinclair was certainly in a position to understand her daughter's desire to marry a much older man. In the end, it may have been this understanding that enabled the mother to overcome her grave reservations about the marital match.

But the story gets ahead of itself. The teacher's pet, the errand-runner, was turning into a bit of a tomboy. Although she made friends easily with girls, Margaret loved playing cowboys and Indians and rough-housing with the boys in the neighborhood. At the age of eleven or twelve, no one would have recognized in this wild-haired, war-whooping child the beautiful, ultrafeminine woman that she would become in half-a-dozen years. Throughout the tomboy stage she continued to be an excellent student, bringing home glowing report cards that dwelled upon her abilities as an actress and her good progress in French, studies that undoubtedly stood her in good stead a little later in life.

Margaret's transformation from tomboy to young lady was gradual and natural. Along with the rest of her sisters, she was learning the basics of cooking from a fine teacher—her mother. The early cooking lessons took hold, for she soon became an excellent cook. Later on, she was confident enough of her abilities to bake her own wedding cake, and as a young bride she won praise for her delicate cuisine. Mrs. Sinclair also insisted (since she had neither servants nor cleaning women) that her daughters all pitch in with the housework.

Part of the polishing process was dancing lessons. Margaret attended every week with a friend, studying all the ballroom steps as well as tap dancing. The lessons were enjoyable but it seems Margaret did not always take them very seriously. Often she and her friends were up to mischief, breaking the rules by bringing in cookies to the studio and getting caught eating them on the sly instead of paying attention.

She was more conscientious, though, about other feminine skills. At Hamilton Junior Secondary School she learned to sew during a home economics course and did so well at it that later she seriously considered a career in fashion design. Although she has not pursued this early interest, she did retain her skill and not only designed, but also made her own wedding dress.

The high school where Margaret was enrolled

had a reputation throughout Vancouver for its strict academic standards and rather restrictive code of behavior. Most of its students came from upper-middle-class, North-Vancouver families. Margaret's three older sisters had preceded her at the school, and like them she had sailed through with ease. High school was primarily a time for testing all of the social skills.

In only a few years, Margaret had changed from a tomboy into a stunning young woman. She turned heads just by walking past the boys as they fetched books from their lockers. Already she had an air of distinction about her. Most of her male classmates admired her from a distance, knowing without being told that she was beyond their reach.

It was the early part of the sixties, and there was no hint yet of the rebellion, the "turn on-tune in-drop out" message that later spread like wildfire through the high schools and universities. At Delbrook High there was a strict message: no bluejeans in school and no smoking on the grounds, on threat of expulsion. Was it rebellion against these rigid standards that led Margaret, only a few years later, to become addicted to both bluejeans and cigarettes? While she attended the school, she certainly showed no signs of discomfort or rebellion. If anything, she seemed eager to conform, to fit in, to excel at popularity.

And Margaret, so successful at so much that she attempted, succeeded here as well. Although she kept aloof from most of the boys in her classes, there were always a number who met her approval and who therefore gave her a choice of dates. Invariably, they were polite, well-groomed young men who brought her home in time for the strict midnight curfew her parents had set. Her life was not, however, a constant whirl of dating. For one thing, she was serious about her schoolwork and spent many hours at home hitting the books. On Saturdays, she worked as a teen fashion counsellor at a Vancouver department store—a much-coveted job that was given to only the most attractive and popular students.

While most of the boys in her classes got the cold shoulder from Margaret, she had developed a passionate teenage crush on an American visitor, one of a group of exchange students who had attended classes at Delbrook High for about two weeks. Margaret's best girlfriend had also developed a crush on one of the other visiting students. By the end of the two weeks, Margaret and her friend had become quite attached to these boys and when they left, the girls were devastated. Convinced that the love of her life had been thwarted, Margaret pleaded with her parents until she was given permission to visit the boys. Ecstatic, she set off with her girlfriend for a weekend train trip to the boys' home town of Portland, Oregon, their excitement growing steadily as the train covered the miles of track. They were met at the station by their respective boyfriends, but for Margaret the reunion was an anticlimax. She quickly realized that the romance back in Vancouver had been lent a false passion and intensity by the anticipation that it would soon end. She and her friend were taken around Portland by the boys to see the sights but the young Sinclair girl found it almost a chore. When the weekend was over, Margaret was happy to leave.

The turning point in the life of Margaret Sinclair was the summer of 1965—the summer after her graduation from high school. It was the mid-point of the decade, the dividing line between the staid era of short hair for boys, skirts for girls, and obedience to authority, and that troubled period when the post-war babies came into their own. In her graduating class yearbook Margaret declared that she intended to spend a year in Switzerland and then pursue a career in fashion design. In fact, she did neither.

Instead, she spent the summer in Vancouver where change was in the air, inevitably drifting up from progressive California. Something was happening in California, in the streets of San Francisco, and on the campus at Berkeley. Tens of thousands of youths were leaving their parents' homes in prosperous suburbs all over North America in a pilgrimage to the west coast. They came to listen to rock bands that sprang up overnight, playing odd, disturbing melodies and singing lyrics about drugs, peace and love. They smoked grass and dropped acid and panhandled spare change on street corners. At Berkeley, students began occupying buildings, staging angry demonstrations, demanding that the administration turn over to them control of courses, saying that most of what they were being taught was dangerous lies. Berkeley set the tone for universities all across the continent.

Was it a reaction against the strict confines of high school, the restrictions her parents placed upon her at home? Or was it just a natural curiosity, a desire to peer outside the small circle of friends, family and conventions that had been her life for so long? Whatever the cause, the most serious disagreement that Margaret and her parents had ever had took place at that time. Margaret wanted to go to Berkeley. Her father was dead set against the idea. The battle raged for several days, but Jimmy Sinclair had the upper hand. He paid the bills, and he would not pay for Berkeley.

As a compromise, Margaret decided to enroll at Simon Fraser, the futuristic university that had just opened its doors on top of Burnaby Mountain, near Vancouver. With its ready-made radicalism, complete with sit-ins and left-wing militancy, Simon Fraser had rapidly become known as Canada's Berkeley. So, in a sense, Margaret got her way. Fascinated with the rough-and-ready radical politics of many of her fellow students, she nonetheless remained an observer, not a participant. She decided to major in Sociology, but also studied English Literature intensively. The innocence-and-experience poems of William Blake affected her profoundly, and she absorbed their message. From reading Blake's poetry and basking in the peace/love philosophy that abounded at Simon Fraser,

Margaret was emerging as a flowerchild, not yet ready to live out on the streets, but quite ready to move out of home.

Soon after entering university, she moved into a large old co-operative house with a young British couple, Mike Mulkay, a teaching associate in Sociology at the university, and his wife Lucy. While staying with the Mulkays, Margaret met Phil Stanworth, another resident of the house. Stanworth, who had come from England to do graduate work at Simon Fraser, was four years older than Margaret, had long hair and a beard, and had a deep commitment to radical politics. Perhaps because he was so completely different from any of the boys she had dated in high school, Margaret was strongly attracted to the cool, reserved Englishman. And gradually his reserve melted in turn. They began an intense relationship, much to the dismay of her parents who did not approve of Stanworth's appearance, or for that matter, his politics. The young couple rarely visited the Sinclairs together, for Margaret was only too aware of her parents' disapproval.

The affair lasted eighteen months. It was the most intense involvement Margaret had ever had with radical politics, but she still refrained from taking an active part herself. Simon Fraser was a time for learning and experimentation, and it was there that Margaret smoked marijuana for the first time. Like many other students she casually adopted marijuana, using it in much the same way that an older generation had used alcohol on social occasions. Stanworth and four other teaching assistants at Simon Fraser became radical celebrities in 1967 when they were fired from their jobs for taking part in demonstrations at a high school in Vancouver, where a student had been suspended for circulating a leaflet criticizing a teacher. By this time, however, Margaret had begun to drift away from the English activist, at least partly because she did not share his commitment to politics.

That year, 1967, was the same year that a politician entered Margaret's life for the first time.

3
Courtship:
Pierre meets Margaret

The courtship of Margaret Sinclair, lovely, wealthy flowerchild, seems more a vignette from a pocket romance than an incident from real life. Margaret, aged nineteen and filled with the theories that three years of intense university study develops, entered the pages of popular romance on the hot sands and calm waters of Mooréa, a tiny, exclusive island resort in the Pacific, twelve miles northwest of Tahiti. Life on the beautiful island is languid, and although progress—in the form of several posh restaurants and cottage-style hotels for tourists—has put its stamp on Mooréa, there is none of the vulgar hustle-bustle of the Caribbean resorts. One hotel manager has said that although he needs fifty employees, he hires one hundred, because at least half of the workers never show up for work. The island's most profitable resource is its natural beauty; only wealthy tourists can afford to sample its fabulous delights.

Most people who visit this remote Pacific island are travelers bound for Australia or New Zealand. A Canadian who makes the long air journey to Mooréa is usually a seasoned traveler who has seen just about every other vacation resort in the world. He must also be well-to-do, because most materials and many foodstuffs must be imported at great expense. James Sinclair, a former Liberal Cabinet Minister who since leaving politics had done well as an executive in Vancouver, was vacationing there in December, 1967 with his wife and three of their five daughters. His second-youngest daughter, Margaret, devoted her time to absorbing the sun and trying to assimilate the teachings of the poets and philosophers who were beginning to have a profound effect upon her.

In the middle of her relaxation and reflections, she came upon an intense man with the body of an athlete and the mind of a scholar. Rather, he chanced upon her. Pierre Elliott Trudeau was forty-eight and, after three years in federal politics, Justice Minister of Canada. Despite the brevity of his time in political office, he had already become a household word across ten provinces for his outspoken utterances, his sometimes unusual dress, his devastating wit and intellect, and his fabled personal charm. He was also perhaps the most eligible bachelor in Canadian political history, worth, at a modest estimate, about $5 million. He had inherited this fortune from his father, a lawyer who had made his name before and during the Depression in a string of service stations in Quebec.

Parliament had recessed for the Christmas holidays, Prime Minister Lester Pearson had announced he was going to retire, and the Justice Minister had jetted to Mooréa to mull over the possibility of running for the leadership of the Liberal party. In going to Mooréa, he had demonstrated how different he was, how aloof he was from most of his Cabinet colleagues who were taking in the sun in more pedestrian places like Florida. Traveling with two friends, Trudeau had booked into the posh Club Méditerranée on Mooréa. The Sinclairs were also staying at the Club Med, and it was only natural that a past and a present Liberal Cabinet Minister should strike up an acquaintanceship.

Mrs. Sinclair, even after her many years as a political wife, was very excited about meeting Pierre Trudeau. In the middle of one idyllic afternoon, in the timelessness of the island, she rushed up to her sun-tanned daughter and effused, "Oh, Margaret, do you know who I've just seen?" Margaret listened, polite but pre-occupied, as Mrs. Sinclair talked rapidly, almost breathlessly, about "Pierre Trudeau, the Justice Minister of Canada — here!" But, basically, Margaret could not have cared less. "I wasn't very much interested in politicians at that time and I wasn't very impressed." She forgot her mother's prattling while she tried to master the more important intricacies of water skiing.

"There was a raft out in the middle of the lagoon," she recalled later, "and this man came and sat down and waited his turn. He gave me a few tips because I didn't know much about water skiing and then he went off on the skis and I was watching him—he was very good."

The setting—a bobbing raft on the deep blue waters of the lagoon—was dazzling, and the sun was almost hypnotic. Margaret felt something close to enchantment about the moment, and something close to magic about the mysterious stranger who seemed to carry with him an aura of enormous accomplishment and extraordinary promise. She did not know until her mother told her later that the man was Pierre Trudeau, and she was surprised to learn that he was a politician —one of those creatures who had not interested her at all. Not knowing anything about him except that he was good with water skis, her attitude towards Trudeau was instinctive, not reasoned. Later, she put it like this: "We started talking about everything from revolutions to Plato to Blake, and just to ordinary things like water skiing and skin diving. And I was very, very impressed with him, very fond of him . . . very fond of him."

When Margaret talked about this meeting a few years after she had been married, it was in the calm, confident tones of a woman secure in her relationship with her husband. But at the time she felt that her attraction to him was not reciprocated. Pierre Trudeau quickly assumed the role of a favorite uncle to the three vacationing Sinclair girls, chatting and joking with them and giving them pointers on all of the skills one must have to pursue leisure successfully on the island.

Although he confided later that he had decided almost immediately that Margaret was the woman he would marry—if he married at all —the Justice Minister kept his own counsel at the time. The two friends traveling with him had no inkling that he was beginning to fall in love. A long-time acquaintance says that Pierre Trudeau "has no capacity for intimacy. He is a wonderful conversationalist on abstract topics, but anything intimate is taboo. Besides, his attitude towards women is strange."

Trudeau had already dated some of the most beautiful women in Canada, but even his closest friends knew little about his personal life. Thus, his approach to Margaret was quite in keeping with his past habits. So successfully did he conceal his feelings from her that she did not expect to see him ever again. She had no thought of marriage at that time, to Pierre Trudeau or to any other man, considering herself "very young". But Trudeau had excited Margaret's curiosity, and she interpreted his off-hand attitude as a sign of complete lack of interest.

The idyllic holiday soon ended and Pierre Trudeau and the Sinclairs returned separately to Ottawa and to Vancouver. It had been a pleasant, even exciting encounter for the Sinclairs; but it had also seemed, like so many acquaintanceships struck up while vacationing, to have ended as quickly as it had begun. Still turning over the possibilities of contesting the leadership of the Liberal Party, Pierre Trudeau temporarily set aside thoughts of the lovely nineteen-year-old who had impressed him so forcefully. Margaret resumed university life. Her regret at parting was as deep as her conviction that she would never see the fascinating older man again.

On Moeréa she had learned little about Pierre Trudeau. Back in Vancouver, the newspapers were full of stories about him—first the speculation that he was a strong contender to succeed Lester Pearson, next the confirmation that he would run, and finally his easy victory in the leadership race.

Margaret learned that he had grown up almost in the style of an aristocrat, being driven, like his older sister, Suzette, and younger brother, Charles, before and after him, to school every day by the family chauffeur, but learning early to be careful with his money. From his days at Jean de Brébeuf classical college in Montreal, he was acknowledged as a brilliant scholar; he had also acquired a reputation as a good scrapper and a person who did not hesitate to pick fights, which he invariably won. By the time he was in his early twenties, people were predicting he would one day be Prime Minister. Margaret learned that like the other members of his family, he was painfully shy, but unlike his brother and sister, he had learned to overcome his shyness, or to mask it behind a brashness that often seemed to be cold, disdainful arrogance.

From about age ten, Trudeau was determined that no one would ever get the better of him, either by cunning or by force, and he embarked on a rigorous program of training that eventually made him an expert in almost every sport or discipline that he tried. He became a brown belt in judo, as well as an excellent skier, boxer, diver and dancer. Margaret also learned that he had been torn between Law and Psychology, and that he had chosen Law because the University of Montreal did not offer courses in Psychology. The Second World War did not permit him to leave the country, but as soon as the war was over, he more than compensated for this travel restriction, taking a Master's degree in Political Economy at Harvard and following that up with classes in Paris as the Ecole des Sciences Politiques and the Law faculty of the Sorbonne. In England, he enrolled at the London School of Economics.

She learned, too, about a wanderlust that had set in after ten years of study, a wanderlust that drove him, with a few necessities stowed in a packsack, across five continents, traveling with down-and-outers on cargo ships or hitchhiking across more than twenty countries. Always, in his travels, his studies and later, in his writing (in a Montreal left-of-center magazine called *Cité Libre*), it was politics that fascinated Trudeau. He had grasped the mechanics of politics in Canada during two years as an adviser to the Privy Council Department in Ottawa, but once that had been learned, he had grown bored and

turned once again to writing, occasionally prac-
ticing labor law and more frequently wandering
the globe. He became a teacher of Constitutional
Law at the University of Montreal in 1962, and
three years later took the plunge into politics: he
was elected a Member of Parliament, made a
Parliamentary Assistant to Prime Minister Pearson and after only one year, appointed Minister
of Justice. Margaret remembered her own distaste for politics, but recalled that it was politics,
or rather, Pierre Trudeau's need to reflect on his
political future, that had taken him to Mooréa in
the first place.

The next time Margaret saw Pierre Trudeau,
he was the Prime Minister of Canada.

4
Morocco:
Mysterious Interlude

Margaret's secretive Morocco trip, which she took after graduation from Simon Fraser in 1969, to this day, remains shrouded in mystery. She has mentioned it occasionally herself, but most of her friends refuse to discuss it. A few facts are certain about the trip though: she became deeply involved with an older man, an Arab, wanted to marry him, and was persuaded or prevented from doing so by her parents. In all, Margaret spent about seven months in warm, distant North Africa, and when she returned, she was very unhappy.

The trip to Morocco in the company of a few friends from Vancouver began in the fall of 1969, after her graduation. The group first visited France and Spain, but later Margaret became dissatisfied and struck off on her own, hitching rides and making new friends. Margaret has since described her travels that year as a "magic trip". Moroccans, she said, responded to her with amazing warmth and kindness. "They have the greatest capacity for loving strangers I have ever seen," Margaret told one friend. "We have too much fear in ourselves to really trust one another like the Moroccans do. Their values are so clearly defined and there is such a strong sense of other, of love, and giving, which I don't think we have developed."

Perhaps the closest Margaret has ever come—however fleetingly—to achieving her ideals of total emancipation and a sense of freedom and personal identity was in faraway Morocco. "I remember sitting on a beach about six o'clock one morning, and I was all alone at the time—I didn't know anyone. I hadn't a friend, although I could see a lot of young people around in the area. And there was a grand feeling of being for the first time in my life absolutely free. Nobody knew where I was. My family knew I was in Morocco, but they didn't know exactly where. My friends weren't around. It was like suddenly I was free of anyone's expectations of the person I was. I could just live for the moment. I think that's kind of what I pursued for the next seven months in Morocco."

Whatever it was that made Margaret pursue that freedom necessarily involved removing herself from her family, her friends and her home. Morocco, on the north-western corner of Africa, is almost half way around the world—just about as far as Margaret could get from Vancouver. Why did she want to separate herself by so many

miles? Why does she refuse to divulge her
activities during those seven months on a foreign,
exotic continent?

When her parents did write to her, asking that
she look up a couple from Toronto—old family
friends who were traveling through northern
Africa—Margaret ignored the request. Her mind
was elsewhere, perhaps concerned with the man
she was in love with or perhaps simply learning
to live by the Moroccan mode of life—the slow
sense of time, no feeling of rush, a sense of one-
ness with the world not commonplace in North
America.

One of the few stories which she does tell of
her trip to Morocco is about what she refers to
as her "magic sandals".

Margaret's "magic sandals" were, she said,
"sandals that laced up to my knee and . . . kept
falling down. One day I was walking along with
a friend who had been telling me all his woes
and that he really needed some money to help
out his brother, who had just written to him and
was in a jam. And I said, 'Oh, well, let's not
think about it.' We walked down to the beach
and passed the American Express office and right
out in front of the American Express office my
sandals, both sandals, fell down and I said, 'Well,
let's just sit down and do them up.' And he said,
'I'll just go in and see if I've got any mail.' And
we went in and he had a letter from a friend
with a hundred dollars in it. He said, 'You should
start looking at those sandals, maybe they're
trying to tell you something.'

"And by gosh, you know, I would find that they would start falling down when I'd be going along the street and I should have turned right and I turned left because if I turned right a friend would have been waiting for me. But I turned left, my sandals would fall down, I'd quickly do them up and turn right and there I'd find my friend. It became just such a joke between my friend and me, of those crazy sandals and 'Margaret, what are you doing wrong, your sandals keep falling down.' But that was probably coincidence that the sandals would fall down just when I should take time to think about things but I don't, I'm not ever going to believe that. It was too real and it was just happening too often. I think there are things like that in life that do teach you."

But, other than this one story of "magic sandals", Margaret Trudeau simply will not reveal what had made her stay in Morocco for seven long months. One can only surmise, as one friend of Margaret's did, that it was a strong attraction to outsiders and a desire to experience something other than the normal Canadian lifestyle which had attracted Margaret so strongly. If this is the case, more questions arise: why did she not stay in Morocco, how did her love affair there with the elusive Arab end, and what was Margaret's relationship with other traveling North Americans?

Answers to these and other questions regarding her trip to Africa simply are not forthcoming. One day Margaret Sinclair simply returned to

North America and resumed her life where she
had left it.

*'It's Margaret, Mr. Trudeau...
long distance!'*

5

Marriage:
Secrets Revealed

After Morocco, her romance ended and her quest for spiritual meaning seemingly a failure, Margaret had a difficult time readjusting to Vancouver. Depressed, feeling the effects of culture shock in the staid surroundings of her parents, despairing that her past was worthless and her future not worth thinking about, she moved in with her maternal grandmother, Rose Barnard. Between grandmother and granddaughter there was an extraordinary closeness, and Mrs. Barnard offered Margaret unquestioning comfort and support. Margaret kept in touch with her parents, but spent most of her time trying to come to grips with her feelings. This period in her life was the first tempering of the fiery-forged idealism of her Simon Fraser days, and she sought to banish the sometimes overwhelming effects of a weariness with the world that transcended her physical age. In long walks by herself along the ocean, she found, in the Pacific waves, a physical expression of her turmoil: a process of constant change that returned incessantly to original forms.

In her grandmother's garden she sought to give physical expression to another near-obsession. Spiritual regeneration had eluded her in Morocco, but Margaret began to see in the verdant forms thrusting up from the warm wet soil that self-renewal was possible. Learning from Nature was part of the credo of the youth revolution, and she began to believe that perhaps by making plants grow she could begin to heal herself.

But she was still absorbed in despondency when her mother called to say that the Prime Minister wanted to have dinner with her. So complete had her withdrawal from the world become that she refused at first to meet him. Cajoled by her mother, however, she at last decided to go. They began talking about what she should wear, and Margaret hedged, saying her wardrobe was rags (and it was, almost literally). Mrs. Sinclair, feeling Margaret would get a lift from the excitement of dining with Pierre Trudeau because of his electric celebrity, and also because she remembered how much Margaret had been taken with him, offered to select a suitable outfit. With impeccable taste Mrs. Sinclair selected a white dress and shawl. Margaret looked demure, and only her lustrous coloring and her youth saved her from appearing matronly.

It was August 8, 1970 and the sun shone. After calling for her, the Prime Minister took Margaret for a ride on the Grouse Mountain skyride. Later, they sat at a window seat in the Grouse Nest on the mountain overlooking Vancouver. Reporters quickly got word that Pierre Trudeau was dating a beautiful redhead. He told them later he had been out with a "Miss Patterson".

The three-hour dinner was scarcely a private affair, with two RCMP officers hovering nearby. However, the Prime Minister did his best to keep the date as secret as possible. He cancelled a planned motorcycle escort, and borrowed a car for the evening. Throughout dinner they were very quiet and their waiter recalled only that they were "nice people to serve". In contrast to Margaret's modest apparel, her escort was dressed so extravagantly, in a blue suit with an open shirt and yellow, western style scarf, that he was worried he might not be allowed into the restaurant. Setting out with the Prime Minister, Margaret felt uncomfortable in her new outfit, feeling almost as though she had put on a disguise. But, as she recalled later, "He spotted me right through it." To her surprise, Margaret enjoyed herself thoroughly and the fascination she had felt for the mysterious man who had coached her in water skiing was rekindled. However, when the inevitable reporters showed up, impatient for the complete story on her date with the Prime Minister, she said noncommittally that the evening had been "very pleasant", but that

she and Mr. Trudeau were just friends. Her reply
was in marked contrast to a date the Prime
Minister had had earlier in the year while attending the Commonwealth Conference. The woman,
an unnatural blonde, had confessed to the world
after a chaperoned lunch with the Prime Minister
that it had been "love at first sight".

For Margaret, at that point, it certainly was
not love. But she was interested again, and it
was clear that Trudeau was too. Before the two
RCMP officers drove her home, Pierre and
Margaret had agreed to see each other again.

Although they rarely appeared in public
together, the two became almost inseparable.
There were long walks together in the woods and
the mountains around Vancouver, and much
serious conversation. Mrs. Sinclair became concerned that Margaret's relationship with this
much older man was fraught with danger. James
Sinclair was concerned as well, and at first was
perhaps a little cool towards the unlikely suitor,
a middle-aged bachelor with a reputation for
dalliances, but a marked reluctance to become
seriously involved with any of his many beautiful
dates. Finally he resolved the matter by telling
himself that his daughter was headstrong and
would do what she wanted in spite of anything
her parents, or anyone else might say.

The Sinclairs were not alone in their reservations about the wisdom of the relationship. Pierre
Trudeau was fascinated by his companion's
beauty, and he found her naïveté charming; but
what was particularly drawing him closer to

Margaret was her incredible idealism. He felt sometimes as though he could look at her and see a part of himself, a part that had not disappeared, but that had been submerged, as a protection against the grossness, the expediency, and the compromise of political life. And more, he saw a sweet wisdom in this young woman, a wisdom rooted not in experience but in intuition: that pure wisdom of a child. As a teenager in Montreal in the late 1930s, Pierre Trudeau had gone on the occasional date, but a contemporary recalls that his behavior was always extremely formal. A date with a girl consisted mostly of dinner and conversation. He refrained from almost any display of affection. Most of his dates were not even asked for a goodnight kiss at the door.

Now, thirty years later, he had an opportunity to relive part of his youth. There is no doubt that Margaret attracted him more powerfully than any woman ever had before. But Trudeau's reason fought against compulsion, and against Margaret's desire for a permanent relationship. The one incontrovertible fact was that he was twenty-nine years older than she. It was like this: he was two years older than Margaret's mother, and had a niece, his sister Suzette's daughter, who was only a year older than Margaret. One of Pierre Trudeau's strongest traits, and at times one of his largest obstacles—is his pride. He could hear the sly remarks about May-September marriages, could imagine reporters conjecturing about Margaret being still a young woman when he reached his dotage. There was the risk of humiliation, of being cuckolded. Some people, including a few Liberal insiders, speculated that such a marriage would be political suicide for him. Perhaps more importantly to Trudeau, there was a conviction that despite the strong mutual attraction, the match was doomed to failure because of the wide gulf in experience that stood between them.

It was up to Margaret, then, to take the initiative of bringing about a marriage. She explained that marriage, children, security, and a domestic union were extremely important to her. She emphasized their similarities; gradually the edges of the outside world went out of focus, leaving them standing together, standing apart, sharing a vision of their relationship and of Canada, an understanding of their own destiny and that of the country of which Pierre Trudeau was Prime Minister and that no one else could quite comprehend. It was a storybook courtship, unprecedented for a Canadian Prime Minister.

Gradually, over several months, Margaret and Pierre came to an understanding. Encircled by love, they decided defiantly to outface the world. Any apprehensions or hints of opposition served only to draw them closer. Theirs was an understanding too fine for others to comprehend; Margaret assured Pierre that they could endure together, and he believed her. By the end of the summer of 1970 they were talking seriously about marriage. In Margaret's eyes, the agreement amounted to a formal engagement, although the Prime Minister never thought of it as such.

Soon after the dinner date in Vancouver, Margaret moved to Ottawa to be close to the Prime Minister. She took a research job with the federal Department of Manpower and Immigration, a job she thoroughly disliked, because it stuck her in an office all day. It was almost a schizophrenic existence: studying the problem of chronic unemployment in an obscure civil-service office by day, and at night being squired around by the most famous man in Canada. Occasionally, they appeared in public—in one instance they were highly visible at a formal evening at the National Arts Centre. But most of the time it was quiet meetings at 24 Sussex, or in her posh apartment in the Rockcliffe Arms, an Ottawa landmark that has since been torn down to make way for skyscrapers.

With marriage firmly in her mind, Margaret returned to Vancouver to make preparations. Pierre Trudeau was a quietly devout Catholic and Margaret was raised an Anglican. She decided she must convert to Catholicism and searched until she found a progressive-minded priest. She picked Father John Swinkels, pastor of St. Stephen's, an upper-middle-class parish in North Vancouver. At forty-two, the Dutch-born Father Swinkels seemed to be exactly what Margaret was looking for: he was discreet and didn't mind rushing the process of conversion.

The priest later said Margaret had a good mind and was always prepared for the instruction, and "with someone like that, one may proceed a bit faster."

Margaret struck Father Swinkels as being "an intellectual" who seemed to have done some reading on conversion on her own. While she was receiving instruction from him, Margaret did not seem at all young. Rather, she struck him as a mature woman who knew exactly what she was doing. Margaret was received into the Catholic faith in February, 1971, about two weeks before her marriage.

The wedding ceremony at St. Stephen's Roman Catholic Church in North Vancouver was booked for several months in advance, but Father Swinkels was told only that Margaret was marrying a man named Mercier from France. Three days before the wedding he was let in on the secret. With the disclosure came the request that he obtain special dispensation from his bishop to forego the publishing of the banns. He agreed. So secretive was Margaret herself that three of her sisters did not know about the wedding until they were about to leave for the ceremony. Her mother, and sister, Rosalind, the bridesmaid, had been told in September, but even her father was not informed until December. On the wedding day, March 4, 1971, to camouflage the true purpose, the sisters were gathered in the living room of the Sinclair home and told that a photographer was coming to take a picture commemorating the sixtieth anniversary of the arrival in Canada of James Sinclair, at age two, from Scotland.

Margaret had designed and sewn her own wedding dress. It was inspired by the garments she had seen in Morocco: floor-length, white, and in a loosely woven Finnish wool. Her sisters were incredulous at the inappropriateness of the garment and one said: "You don't wear a dress like that for a family picture." Another chimed in: "Are you a kook? You look like you're going to a wedding." Then, of course, they realized the truth.

Pierre Trudeau had been similarly secretive. In Ottawa he informed members of his Cabinet that he was going skiing for a few days on the west coast. As the Government JetStar aircraft he was traveling in passed over Alberta, he changed into a morning suit. When he landed at Vancouver, he and his executive assistant, Gordon Gibson, were taken in an unmarked police car to the church. Mr. Gibson learned the purpose of the trip from the Prime Minister's off-hand observation, "You're not very well dressed for a wedding."

The wedding license had been obtained surreptitiously by James Sinclair. Realizing that word would get out immediately if he got it in Vancouver, Mr. Sinclair went to the small town of Squamish, twenty-nine miles from the city. An RCMP staff sergeant issued it. Told the groom's name, the Mountie became so nervous that his hands began to shake. However, when he came to the space on the form for the groom's profession, he wrote "Prime Minister" without prompting. Margaret paid the license fee herself.

Fourteen people attended the secretive forty-five-minute nuptial Mass: Margaret's parents and four sisters; her brother-in-law, Tom Walker, assistant football coach at Simon Fraser; the Prime Minister's brother and best man, Charles; Charles' wife, Andree; the priest, organist and photographer. The Prime Minister's mother, Grace Elliott Trudeau, who had been ill for years, did not attend, but her son telephoned her from the reception. His sister, Suzette, and her husband and children were unable to reach their plane in Montreal because of a blizzard.

In the church, the excited and nervous organist improvised on sacred themes and the wedding began. The soon-to-be famous couple exchanged antique gold rings and then received Communion. Margaret Sinclair became Mrs. Pierre Trudeau, the youngest wife of a Prime Minister in Canadian history, and also the youngest wife of any political leader in the western world.

The wedding reception was held at the Capilano Golf and Country Club. While the Sinclairs and Trudeaus celebrated quietly, club members in other rooms sipped at their drinks, chatted and played cards, oblivious to the historic occasion. Margaret and her husband joined hands to cut a three-tiered wedding cake she had baked. The guests dined on turtle soup and chateaubriand, toasting the newlyweds with Piper Heidsieck champagne. When Heather Sinclair's husband, Tom Walker, proposed the toast to Margaret, Trudeau was uncharacteristically struck for a reply. He made a few false starts, then confessed,

"I don't know what to say." Janet Sinclair half-humorously, half-impatiently, remembered the Prime Minister's famous euphemism which had caused a sensation in the House of Commons. "Why don't you say 'fuddle-duddle'," she suggested.

The marriage would have been a complete secret, but for the excitement of one of Margaret's sisters, who could not refrain from telling her friends at the country club the exciting news. A small crowd had gathered outside by the time the wedding party left the building.

The new wife's honeymoon wardrobe consisted of her ski clothes. The newlyweds spent a long weekend at the Sinclair family's condominium at Whistler Mountain, but only after the flustered groom had returned to Vancouver to fetch the keys he'd forgotten for the honeymoon home. After four days on the slopes, Margaret and Pierre Trudeau flew back to Ottawa to begin married life at 24 Sussex Drive.

The first few months as wife of the Prime Minister were confusing and exciting, as was only to be expected. News of the marriage aroused intense curiosity and Margaret immediately found herself the subject of several magazine articles, which probed her past, her personality, her family and her possibilities. The marriage itself was the subject of a *Time* magazine cover story ("Pierre and Margaret: Minds of their Own") which said she was "most frequently described in terms that suggested that she is a cross between Doris Day and the Flying Nun."

Time also set the tone for the newspaper and magazine stories that followed about the "flower-child who married the Prime Minister" by quoting someone as saying "Marg is a hippie in spirit, and I mean that referring to all the best things about hippies."

Reporters, right from the beginning, found it tough going: family members said they had been instructed that all information about their affairs must come from the Prime Minister's Office. Friends in Vancouver maintained a tight-lipped loyalty, and few people in Ottawa knew anything about the young bride.

Margaret had prepared herself for the role of wife to Pierre Trudeau, but not for that of wife of the Prime Minister. At official receptions, she clung to her husband for support. She felt completely alien to political life, and ignored most of the offers of help or friendship from the wives of top Liberals, feeling they were not genuine. Almost immediately, she decided she would stay out of politics. She stuck to her resolve most of the time, but was to break it when the Prime Minister was campaigning for his political life in the hard-won federal election of 1974.

The Trudeaus' first public appearance was three weeks after their marriage when they attended a maple-sugar party in the small community of St. Joseph du Lac about twenty-five miles northwest of Montreal. Margaret was the hit of the party, receiving and returning congratulatory kisses from members of the sponsoring Liberal Party association from her husband's

Montreal riding of Mont-Royal. Dressed in blue-jeans, a white turtleneck sweater and a yellow ski jacket, Margaret gamely tried a lively French-Canadian square dance. The dancing was so strenuous that her toque kept falling off, and at times she was confused by the rapid-fire instructions of the caller. She ate a hearty meal of pea soup, beans and an omelet laced with fresh maple sugar and then went for a sleigh ride, taking a turn at the reins of the two horses.

Although the party was friendly, things became a bit frightening as the guests scrambled to get a close look at the couple. It had been arranged that the Trudeaus would mingle and try to meet and talk with as many people as possible, but the situation threatened to get out of hand as the 600 guests refused to stay in small groups. Members of the Prime Minister's staff went through an exhausting workout making sure the couple didn't get trampled. But Pierre, dressed in bluejeans and a buckskin jacket, stayed close to his beautiful wife, lending her encouragement as she chatted.

Despite the precautions taken to keep the visit a secret, word spread and motorists converged on the scene, causing a traffic jam on the highway as they waited to catch a glimpse of the Trudeaus. To oblige them, the couple spent ten minutes waving and talking to the party-crashers before departing to spend the weekend in Montreal.

It was the first time in her young life that Margaret had ever received so much attention.

It must have been an exhilarating, exciting and frightening experience. Some say, in light of her actions later in the marriage, that she was a publicity seeker from the start. Certainly, this early taste of celebrity must have had a profound effect on the woman.

Ten days after this appearance, the Trudeaus were off to the Caribbean for a two-week Easter vacation, far away from the prying eyes of the Canadian public. In a continuation of their brief British-Columbia honeymoon, they visited several of the islands before the Prime Minister had to return to Ottawa for the reconvening of the House of Commons. Early in May, the Trudeaus returned to Vancouver for the visit of Queen Elizabeth of England, her husband, Prince Philip, and her daughter, Princess Anne. The arrival of the Trudeaus at Vancouver Airport attracted as much attention as did the royal family when their jet touched down ten minutes later. Standing in a crowd that included the Governor-General of Canada and the Lieutenant-Governor and Premier of British Columbia, Margaret showed daring by wearing a mid-length, brown and black checked dress with puffed sleeves. The Queen and Princess Anne wore dresses with hemlines just below the knees.

Before her marriage, Margaret had been told by Pierre to prepare for a springtime tour of Russia. In late September, 1970, she paid a visit to the small shop of Peter Plunkett-Norris, an exclusive Vancouver dress designer, in preparation for the trip.

"A dark-haired girl walked into my salon and wanted an extensive trousseau wardrobe because she was marrying a diplomat and would be living in the East," Plunkett-Norris recalls. She explained she would be going on a tour of Russia with her husband shortly after she was married and that some of her clothes must be Russian-oriented. "I didn't know her at all but her name was Margaret Sinclair."

Margaret had strolled in wearing bluejeans, a white, faded T-shirt and a long macintosh with a pin securing a torn pleat at the back. The dress designer thought she looked very young, anywhere from fourteen to twenty years old and with her square, smoked lens granny glasses, it was hard to tell. At first Mr. Plunkett-Norris thought it was a gag, perhaps a high-school hazing stunt.

"She wanted everything mid, her favorite length. Her only stipulation was that nothing be opulent or overly decorative because her husband-to-be was a man of very fine taste and disliked anything ostentatious."

The designer did a series of sketches that were examined by Margaret and her mother. After they had spent four hours choosing fabrics, Mrs. Sinclair asked him not to show anybody the designs and not to tell anyone that Margaret was getting married. "She told me that if I should phone her home to make appointments that I was to be sure to speak only to her daughter or to her. I wasn't even to say who I was if anybody else answered the phone."

Out of the consultations came a twelve-piece trousseau of day and evening wear for Margaret, including a coat of royal blue and rust tapestry, lined and trimmed with ivory fur in a style inspired by the epic film, *Doctor Zhivago*. It came with a reversible babushka made with tapestry on one side and fur on the other. Her evening gown was made from a white sari trimmed with gold, brown, and green border. A leisure outfit consisted of a fringed poncho and matching skirt in handwoven white wool trimmed with dark maroon.

The trousseau also included a five-piece ensemble in golden olive raw silk consisting of a high cutaway coat, high-waisted skirt with suspenders, military pants, vest, and a brown and cream silk print blouse. Guessing the identity of the groom, Plunkett-Norris sewed a tag bearing the initials MT into the label of one of her coats. "The secrecy was so extreme that the groom had to be Pierre Trudeau," he said later.

Pierre Trudeau had visited Moscow to attend a Soviet-sponsored economic conference in 1952, at the height of the Stalinist regime. At that time, he had run into trouble with the authorities for throwing a snowball at a statue of Lenin, and when he returned to Canada, found himself "roundly attacked for being a Communist". Twenty years later, the Prime Minister and his wife received a standing ovation when they attended the Bolshoi Theatre with Soviet Premier Alexei Kosygin. The Trudeaus sat on either side of Premier Kosygin in what had been the Czar's own box when the Bolshoi was built in 1856. Wearing a plain, elegant white dress, and with her hair swept up, Margaret was the object of much curiosity from Russians and visiting Western reporters alike. One Canadian observer remarked that she and the Prime Minister "look enough alike to be brother and sister". The ballet was Swan Lake—the famous dance in which love triumphs over all.

Earlier in the day, Margaret had attended her first official function in Moscow. She visited the Palace of Pioneers, a community center for specially chosen children, in the company of Mrs. Andrei Gromyko, wife of the Soviet Foreign Minister.

She learned that the youngsters at the center, ranging in age from seven to fourteen, were the children of working mothers, and that they stayed at the institute after school. While Margaret was visiting the center, the Prime Minister was holding discussions with the Soviet Premier. At the Palace of Pioneers, Margaret received so many gifts from the children that she had to pass some of them on to an aide to carry.

The next day, Margaret visited a ballet school where she was confronted by a Soviet television crew. As she watched a group of young dancers, she was suddenly blinded by powerful TV lights and exclaimed, "I can't see." She seemed tense and nervous at first, but during the next hour and a half she loosened up. The director of the school, Golovkina Sofi Nikolaevna, said Mrs. Trudeau would make a good Gypsy dancer. George Bain, then Ottawa columnist for the

Toronto *Globe and Mail*, wrote: "One impression —another is that the lady herself is simply prima donnaish—is that someone is being unnecessarily protective of Mrs. Trudeau, not of her personal safety, which isn't being endangered anyway, but of her public image, in case she should make a mistake, or somehow appear gauche."

Mr. Bain went on to note that if Margaret didn't get "an occasional fit of the inner quakes, it would be most surprising. It is some launching into the faintly lunatic world of statecraft to be called upon to perform the sort of public functions that a Prime Minister's wife has to perform in, of all places, Moscow."

After the trip to Russia, Margaret settled in at 24 Sussex with the intention of remaining as much a private person as she could. For the most part she tried to steer clear of her husband's official trips and meetings, since an appearance with him at a public event meant facing the persistent questioning of reporters and the curious stares of just about everyone. She found herself spending most of her time alone, for the Prime Minister had returned to his routine of fifteen-hour days in the House of Commons or his office all day, and meetings with aides, Cabinet Ministers, businessmen and labor leaders at night. She was slow to make friends: most of the wives of her husband's colleagues were women in their forties or older and she did not share their often cynical views about surviving in the protocol-conscious social quagmire of Ottawa. Not wishing to develop a contrived attitude, and warned that honesty and forthrightness lead to trouble, she compromised by saying nothing in public.

After the simple life she had led at her grandmother's house in Vancouver, the elaborate arrangements at the Prime Minister's official residence were overwhelming. Her relationship with the eight servants at 24 Sussex was uneasy. They expected her to direct them, but instead she wanted to befriend them. This led at times to antagonisms. There was nobody around to tell Margaret what to do, and she became confused. The servants were left to make the decisions themselves, to plan the menu, to choose the meals. The only time Margaret really felt comfortable was when she and Pierre were able to slip out unnoticed for a meal at a delicatessan or a movie downtown.

So, even before Margaret became pregnant for the first time, problems were developing. Out of the public's eye the wife of the Prime Minister was experiencing loneliness, alienation, confusion. Throughout this period, though, the public was only aware of the bright, pretty side of Margaret. In the eyes of the millions of Canadians who loved her, Margaret Trudeau was a charming, sophisticated, elegant woman who made Canada more respectable as a world power.

The freedom she had experienced so joyfully in Morocco only a few years earlier was gradually being exchanged for an existence fraught with responsibilities, expectations and demands.

In the summer of 1971, Margaret discovered that she was pregnant.

'Of course you can bring a
stone to dinner, Margaret...or
any other object!'

6

Pregnancies and Childbirth

From the time she was a little girl playing with dolls, Margaret had dreamed of becoming a mother. In her little-girl fantasy world, her dolls became her children, with names, personalities, nap times, tummy-aches. When it came time to set aside her playthings, however, she did not abandon her dreams. The dolls were relegated to the attic, but Margaret's love of children grew as she matured. In her early teens she began sitting for young parents in her neighborhood, as much for the simple pleasure of playing "mother" for an afternoon or evening as for the small sums of money she received from her mother. Her employers noticed that she was a remarkably conscientious sitter; patient to a fault with their children, willing to read or color with the older ones, and not at all reluctant to change a baby's diaper. Until she began to date in her final years of high school, Margaret was always much in demand as a sitter.

When she entered Simon Fraser University, Margaret encountered the poetry of William Blake. The English poet reinforced her fascination with children, gave it a philosophical framework and a better means of expression. In children she began to see more than just wide-eyed bundles of affection; to Margaret they became a touchstone of hope, a symbol of promise that had never been broken by compromise or sullied by worldliness. She took to heart Blake's lines from "Auguries of Innocence":

> He who mocks the infant's faith
> Shall be mocked in Age and Death.
> He who shall teach the child to doubt
> The rotting grave shall ne'er get out.
> He who respects the infant's faith
> Triumphs over Hell and Death.

Marriage brought Margaret the opportunity to translate poetry into reality. As it turned out, the opportunity came much sooner than she expected. In mid-summer, a few months after her marriage, Margaret discovered that she was expecting her first child. The newlyweds had not wasted any time. Pierre Trudeau, for so long Canada's most eligible bachelor, shared Margaret's happy anticipation of parenthood. The couple began shopping for nursery furnishings and were thinking about hiring a nanny. Pierre Trudeau dropped a few broad hints to friends, and during a visit to Toronto, toured a hospital nursery.

It was, with one rather embarrassing exception, a happy, mellow time for Margaret. Carrying a child gave her a profound sense of fulfillment, and as the summer passed she glowed with an almost madonna-like radiance, content in her marriage and the pleasant anticipation of being a mother. She received the best medical care in Ottawa, and rested secure in the knowledge that she was at the peak of health and at the perfect age for bearing children. She glided through the early months of pregnancy with an ease that would be the envy of most expectant mothers.

The shock came in October, when she accompanied the Prime Minister to an official dinner for visiting Soviet Premier Alexei Kosygin. The dinner was held at Government House, the official residence of Canada's Governor-General. Margaret was seated between Mr. Kosygin and Roland Michener, the Governor-General. At the beginning of the dinner Margaret began to feel queasy, but shrugged it off as the nervousness she often felt on such formal occasions. But when the Governor-General rose to make a speech she felt, to her horror, that she was growing weak. "My god," she thought to herself, "I've never fainted in my life." It was the last thing she remembered before losing consciousness, her head landing on her plate. The fainting spell brought an early end to the evening for Margaret, and a resolution to get more rest.

For the next while she avoided the strain and tension of public appearances, staying at home and planning for the arrival of her child. As the holiday season approached she made one exception, appearing with her husband at a Christmas party on December 16 for members of the Liberal Party. On Christmas Day she was admitted to Ottawa Civic Hospital and at 9:27 that night gave birth to a six-pound, nine-ounce son. The Trudeaus had spent weeks discussing names for the child and had finally settled on Justin Pierre, if it was a boy. The Prime Minister had made several suggestions, but the final decision was made by Margaret.

Although the proud parents refused to discuss their son's namesake, it is likely that their choice was inspired by St. Justin, who was born in Jordan around A.D. 100. Born of pagan parents, he was converted to Christianity as a young man and became a wandering teacher and philosopher, who sometimes lectured in Roman classrooms. He was martyred in Rome when he was in his sixties. The name had political appeal as well, containing an echo of the Prime Minister's often-quoted remarks about his vision of a "Just Society" in Canada.

Whatever the origin of his name, Justin contributed to the fairytale atmosphere surrounding his parents' marriage—the famous father, the beautiful young mother, and a Christmas-Day baby. But even before Justin's birth, a Gallup poll had shown that Margaret was firmly established as a famous person in Canada, and well-liked at that. Most of the people questioned in October, 1971, said that they admired her because she was young and beautiful and showed good sense, intelligence and integrity. Others said she was doing a good job with dignity in her role as wife of the Prime Minister. In all, six out of ten Canadians said that she had won their admiration.

Margaret's popularity at that time was greatest with English-speaking Canadians (sixty-five per cent) and lowest among French-Canadians (forty-nine per cent). Of the ten per cent polled who did not admire her, many felt that she had done nothing to warrant admiration, and others objected to her marrying a man more than twice her age.

But the majority was in her favor, and when she gave birth to a beautiful bouncing boy she not only increased the size of her family, but also furthered her popularity.

Justin's birth was a historic occasion in Canada. He was the first child born to the wife of a Prime Minister in office in 102 years—since Agnes Macdonald, the second wife of Canada's first Prime Minister, Sir John A. Macdonald, gave birth to a daughter on Feb. 7, 1869. Agnes Macdonald and Margaret had more than babies in common. The wife of Canada's first Prime Minister showed a sense of flair and adventure that was not rivalled until Margaret became the chatelaine of 24 Sussex Drive. Among Mrs. Macdonald's much-talked-about exploits was a ride she took on the cowcatcher of a locomotive on a trip with her husband, the better, she explained, to get an unobstructed view.

Margaret's October fainting spell had turned out to be an isolated incident in an uncomplicated pregnancy. The birth of Justin was just as uncomplicated and Margaret, remaining steadfast in her devotion to the natural way of doing things, refused a general anesthetic so that she would be awake when she gave birth. Arriving at the hospital on Boxing Day, the Prime Minister told a flock of reporters that he was afraid that Justin "looks like me". Indeed he did. Even at birth Justin had his father's distinctive nose, and as the balding Prime Minister confessed, both father and son had about the same amount of hair.

Very much the proud father, Pierre Trudeau passed out cigars to reporters who crowded around him at the hospital, hoping to pick up scraps of information about the Christmas baby. Obviously in fine humor, he chatted amiably with the press, but said he wished his wife was with him to answer questions about the birth, because he couldn't.

Justin's arrival was yet another momentous event in Margaret's life—another change in what had become since her involvement with Pierre Trudeau a hectic, whirlwind existence. From the obscurity of college life, to Prime Minister's wife, to mother of Canada's most famous child in such a few short years! Fortunately she was shielded, (for a time anyway) from the demands of public

life by her new status as a young mother. People
were naturally curious about "the Christmas
baby", as he was rapidly labelled, but they also
respected a new mother's right to privacy. After
four days in hospital becoming accustomed to
breast-feeding and bathing Justin, she was taken
home by her husband in plenty of time to
prepare for a quiet New-Year's celebration.

A young French-Canadian woman was en-
gaged as Justin's nanny, and under her protective
care he was installed in the nursery at 24 Sussex
Drive. Even with the nanny, though, there was
a lot of work for Margaret to do. Since Justin
was being breast-fed, it was up to her to get up
in the middle of the night when he was hungry.
Also, Margaret felt an obligation to take a hand
in the running of the big rambling old graystone
mansion with its many rooms and fleet of servants. Sometimes it was tiring, but Margaret felt,
in the presence of her devoted husband and
healthy son, more fulfilled than at any time in
her life.

Although Margaret did her best to remain out
of the public eye, both she and her son were
natural newsmakers. Congratulations poured in
to the Prime Minister's residence, and in Parliament, members of all of Canada's four political
parties rose to extend their best wishes. One
member, pushing the point a little, gave his
"most sincere congratulations on the occasion of
this first birth, that happened on the day of an
equally memorable birthday." When he was four

days old, Justin sat on his mother's knee for a portrait by one of Ottawa's top portrait photographers.

Justin's first public appearance, though, was for his christening at a Roman Catholic Church in Ottawa when he was twenty-two days old. It was a typical, frosty, freezing Canadian winter day, nineteen degrees below zero, and Justin was bundled in tasseled shawls for the trip from Sussex Drive to the church. The Trudeaus easily stole the show from two other Ottawa families whose youngest members were being christened at the same time. A Dominican priest, a friend of the Prime Minister's family, performed the ceremony. Tom Walker, the husband of Margaret's sister, Heather, was named Justin's godfather. The Prime Minister's niece, Mrs. Marie Anne Rouleau Danis, was the godmother.

As he grew older, Justin acquired a reputation for rambunctiousness, perhaps encouraged by his indulgent father, who doted on his son and seldom restrained him. More worrisome for Margaret, though, was the attention lavished upon him by well-meaning servants, visitors and relatives. In no time at all Justin learned he could get around his mother's firm "no" by appealing to the cook, or anyone else who happened to be handy. He was a bright, active child, and from the time he was a few months old, Justin was part of most of the proceedings at the Prime Minister's residence.

At public events, little Justin was often allowed to run around unrestrained. Most of the time people were amused, but occasionally his rowdy behavior caused frowns and a bit of ill feeling.

In August, 1973, four months short of his second birthday, Justin was brought along with his parents to Government House where leaders of British Commonwealth countries were gathered for a reception given by Canada's Governor-General as part of their annual conference. It was a warm summer day, and the guests were gathered on the manicured lawns chatting and sampling refreshments that were being served from a marquee set up in the middle of the green. Justin, barefoot, tore around the lawn putting on a performance for the benefit of his parents and the other guests. The Prime Minister just smiled indulgently as Justin rolled down a hill in the garden at the residence. Margaret, though, was concerned—she chased after the boy, trying to make him behave. The performance did not go over well with all of the guests. One of the assembled heads of state muttered out of earshot of the Trudeaus that he'd had enough of Justin's antics, adding that he thought the child was being exploited unnecessarily by his parents.

By the time of Justin's performance at the Commonwealth conference, Margaret was unknowingly well into her fifth month of pregnancy with her second child. This time her condition was heralded in a highly dramatic fashion, and in a most regal setting. At the end of May, Margaret had accepted an invitation to appear on behalf of her husband at a special Commonwealth Day service on June 1, at Westminster Abbey.

In London, Margaret had caused quite a stir among the British press and public. She was regarded primarily as an object of curiosity because of the great discrepancy between her age and that of the Prime Minister. Pierre Trudeau seemed the most fascinating Canadian the European media had ever encountered, and his wife was of interest mostly because of him.

If this attitude bothered Margaret, she did not allow it to show. When the British newspapers began calling and demanding interviews and photographs, she was most co-operative. In an attempt to forestall pursuit by the press all over London during her visit, she agreed to allow the Fleet Street photographers to take pictures of her at a formal session.

But the majority of her press coverage came later, at the Commonwealth Service at Westminster Abbey. During the ceremony, attended by Queen Elizabeth and Prince Philip, she began to feel a queasiness uncannily similar to the spell she suffered at the Governor-General's reception before Justin was born. As the ceremony in the Abbey ended, and the audience rose while the royal couple made their exit, Margaret suddenly had to sit down and put her head in her lap. The wide-brimmed hat she'd bought for the occasion fell off and was lost in a rush of people. Pulling herself together, Margaret stood up again, but almost immediately fainted and was helped out a side door. Two weeks later she was examined by her physician in Ottawa, who informed her that she was pregnant.

In the fall, during her seventh month of pregnancy, Margaret visited China on an official tour with the Prime Minister. The Chinese openly admired her matter-of-fact attitude towards pregnancy as she traveled about the country with her husband. Premier Chou En-Lai informed Margaret that her visit was an example to Chinese women, whose shamefaced attitude towards pregnancy he thought was old-fashioned and deplorable. He told Margaret that many Chinese women have had themselves transferred to new jobs during their final months of pregnancy to avoid the embarrassment of appearing before their co-workers.

Margaret couldn't have been more off-hand about her condition. During a visit to one of China's most famous landmarks, the Great Wall, she joked with her Chinese companions about her appearance. However, the Prime Minister was especially protective towards her, and would often hold her hand, even when Premier Chou was at his side.

Perhaps because of her condition, Margaret and the Prime Minister were given a tour of a Chinese maternity hospital. It turned out, unfortunately, to be a most bizarre experience. While she was strolling through the wards, a hospital official showed her a six-month-old fetus preserved in a bottle. Displaying commendable restraint, Margaret politely examined the object. Her only comment later was that she found it an odd choice of exhibits for a maternity hospital.

Earlier that year Margaret had said in an interview: "As early as I can remember, I longed, longed to be a mother. But in all your dreams you can't possibly know when you get into it, it is just such a joyful experience. Certainly, I found that pregnancy is just a perfect time in a woman's life because it is just all happy, positive dreams. From the moment I started giving birth to him (Justin) he opened up a completely new world for me, a world that I had been longing for."

Margaret's children were all breast-fed, as she was a strong believer in breast-feeding as well as natural baby foods. Soon after returning from her trip to China, she had another opportunity to experiment with baby-food formulas.

On Christmas Day, 1973, Margaret gave birth to her second son at the same hospital in Ottawa where Justin had been delivered exactly two years earlier. Like his brother, Alexandre Emmanuel was healthy, and his entry into the world was an uncomplicated matter. His father, ever mysterious, gave only a vague explanation for his first name. Facing the inevitable crush of reporters at the hospital, the Prime Minister told them the child was named Alexandre after the saint, the czar or the pope . . . "take the one you want". As for Emmanuel, that was easy. It was, the Prime Minister said, a good biblical name meaning "God is with us", and besides, it was the best Christmas name he could think of. Even before he was taken home from the hospital,

Justin's little brother was given the nickname "Sacha". Early in the new year, Sacha was baptized in a quiet family ceremony in a tiny parish church north of Ottawa.

With two children, there was now even more pressure on Margaret. She regarded Sacha as no less a blessing than Justin but it was another step away from the casual, longed for freedom of life as a single woman, which seemed all the more precious and sweet now that it was gone. For most mothers, caring for two small children is a strain. With all the other pressures in Margaret's life—the politics, the publicity-seekers, the re-sponsibility of running a house that was, with its huge dimensions and staff, more a hotel than a home—the pressure of raising two small children seemed at times a bit too much for her.

Margaret tried to keep a firm hand on Justin, but the baby demanded a lot of her time. More of Justin's care had to be relegated to the nanny and to the other servants. It wasn't an ideal situation—far from it—but Margaret felt power-less to change it. Justin was beginning to show definite signs of an independent spirit, a strong will to have his own way, a trait both his parents obviously possessed. Often, his antics were amus-ing and endearing. But when he threw tantrums at public gatherings because he was overtired or wasn't getting his own way, Margaret felt frus-trated, more sad than angry.

Given this set of circumstances, it is strange to reflect that it was at this time—with pressures at home mounting, and loss of freedom at its peak—that Margaret decided to enter the political world for the first time. It must be understood that little, really, is known about Margaret's life with the Prime Minister before she became a public "personality". To be sure, she was loved and revered before that time, and part of her celebrity was due to the mystique that surrounded her.

But in April, 1974, Margaret Trudeau became a more touchable reality, a person about whom more was known. Let us look then at who this person was and how she dealt with her new toy—power.

7

The Election Trail

It was Margaret's own decision, against the stated intention of her husband and against her own instincts. It was a gamble that paid handsome political dividends. It was also a two-month ordeal that exacted a heavy toll on Margaret's emotional well-being.

Pierre Trudeau declared in 1972 that his wife would never take part in an election campaign because "the whole idea is repugnant to me." That was the year his Liberal Party suffered a humiliating near-defeat at the polls, knocked down to a minority in the House of Commons by voters disenchanted by his seeming arrogance. When the returns came in on election night in 1972, Margaret decided that Canadians did not know the real Pierre Trudeau. She also decided it was her duty to show the country the human side of her husband in the next election campaign.

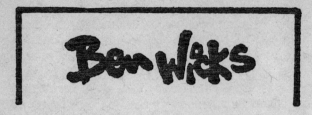

'It's either a campaigning candidate or Margaret Trudeau!'

In April, 1974, before the next election was called, Margaret delivered her first speech—nonpolitical, to be sure, but an unusual occasion nevertheless, because she had remained so much in the background and out of the public eye since her marriage. The occasion was the opening of the new Law building at the University of Ottawa. The reason for her speech was that her husband, scheduled to deliver a speech to mark the event, had unexpectedly had to go to Paris to attend the state funeral of Georges Pompidou, the late French president.

Margaret's pinch-hitting performance attracted an unusually large turnout of about fifty reporters and photographers. Many said they would not have come except for the curiosity of a public appearance by the Prime Minister's usually reclusive wife. Speaking a bit nervously and perhaps a bit too quickly, she accepted an honorary doctoral degree in Law that had been awarded to the Prime Minister and described her task as a "pleasant duty".

The burden of her speech was the apparent contradiction between two goals of the law—the reflection of social change and the upholding of social stability. She asked rhetorically, "Are these attributes incompatible?" and then answered, "In a sense they are, and yet, they must coexist." Perhaps the most impressive part of her performance was not what she had said but how she had said it: some of the passages were in French, a language which she had begun studying seriously only after her engagement to the Prime Minister.

Only once did Margaret lose her poise. A radio reporter adjusting her microphone caused her to falter and lose her place. But, recovering quickly, she won over her audience by looking straight at them with a smile and a shrug. They responded with a companionable chuckle. Afterwards, she admitted that she had been nervous, "but it was all right once I got started."

She had good reason to feel nervous, for her audience was composed largely of legal experts, including Bora Laskin, Chief Justice of the Supreme Court of Canada, and other judges, professors and diplomats. She was congratulated afterwards at a reception by members of the Law faculty, but told them, laughingly, "Don't expect me to go ravaging the country with speeches."

Her intention, in fact, was not to "ravage the country" with eloquence, but to win the hearts and minds of voters with honesty. During the early part of the campaign, through the Atlantic provinces and Quebec, Margaret's role was limited to handshaking, smiling, and generally supporting her husband. Justin, then two years old, stayed at home, but Sacha, aged five months, traveled along. The backroom political strategists Margaret despised so much could not have better planned her contribution. The idea was to soften Pierre Trudeau's harsh image, to present him as a loving husband and a devoted father as well as an astute politician. As the campaign got under way, Margaret seemed omnipresent, watching her husband delivering speeches, her eyes always on him, a smile always on her face.

It worked well for the Prime Minister, but sometimes Margaret felt she was being forced into a role, being portrayed as an incomplete person. She complained that she did not like being packaged as a campaign item, labelled WIFE AND MOTHER.

In Vancouver, she made a speech that became famous for the sexual innuendo some people read into it. Standing on a platform before a crowd of about 2,000 people at a salmon barbecue, she declared that her husband was "quite a beautiful guy . . . who taught me a lot about loving." She was roundly applauded, but the speech also provoked some ribald guffaws and comments. Feeling relaxed before the hometown crowd, she said she had never seen ". . . such friendly faces, such beautiful faces. I want to speak a bit about my husband because I feel I have some inside information." The Prime Minister, she said, had taught her a lot about the love of humanity and about tolerance. Although he was often called arrogant, Margaret said she had found him "shy, modest and very, very kind".

The speech horrified Liberal campaign strategists. Feeling that she had committed a major gaffe and was quite capable of doing so again, party officials told Margaret she should consider having speeches written for her. She rejected the suggestion firmly, saying she would do things her own way, and put her own thoughts into her speeches. At the end of the campaign she turned the seeming gaffe to her advantage by explaining it. Speaking to a crowd of picnickers on Toronto's Centre Island, she said, "I started this campaign by getting into a lot of trouble because I tried to tell people about love and many of them took it the wrong way. But that's about all I can talk about because I really believe in love."

Most of Margaret's truly risqué remarks went unreported. She talked frankly and openly with reporters throughout the campaign, but most of the conversations were understood to be off the record. Even when she didn't specify that her remarks were not for publication, many reporters decided not to quote anything that would reflect unfavorably upon her. She was thought to be politically naïve and unaware of the impact of what she was saying.

During a campaign swing through the Eastern Townships of Quebec, for example, she rode for about two hours in a car with Robert Murdoch, one of her husband's assistants, and a wire-service reporter. She had just put in an exhausting day campaigning and, sitting in the back seat with the reporter, was glad of the opportunity to relax. In the middle of the conversation—scattered observations of no particular consequence —she suddenly said she hoped that her husband would lose the election. Murdoch, sitting in the front seat, was so unnerved by the blurted confession that he turned ashen and began to twitch. Noticing his reaction, Margaret began to hedge a bit. Finally, she said that what she had meant was she hoped if he won, that it would be by a large majority, because she did not want to continue the unhappy, hectic life of the past two years that had been imposed by the minority government situation. Because of that, she would not be unhappy if he lost.

One of the greatest hardships of life on the election trail for Margaret was the separations from her children. She was away from Justin for days at a stretch, seeing him only when she was able to return to Ottawa as the Prime Minister's party traveled through Ontario. Sacha was still being breast-fed at the beginning of the campaign, but midway through it, he had been weaned and Margaret left him with her parents in Vancouver. While traveling, she drew up elaborate schedules showing when and where she would see each of the boys next. June Callwood, a Toronto writer who accompanied Margaret for part of the campaign, wrote in *Maclean's*: "After the first jolt it began to seem commonplace that a baby was traveling on a federal election campaign, his wail of indignation when he was hungry rising over the clatter of typewriters as reporters met deadlines and speechwriters prepared drafts. People on the Prime Minister's tour even grew accustomed to the high comedy of the Trudeau arrivals at airports or train stations. Their bullet-proof limousine would draw up behind the pulsating red lights of a motorcycle escort to be unloaded by burly security men of bassinets, diaper bags, folding strollers and teddybears, while Sacha in his mother's arms watched the scene with round blue eyes."

Miss Callwood, who has spent some time

chatting with Margaret, says that Margaret has an innocence that often shields her. "People develop almost a sense of superiority about her. They are almost co-opted into being her protec-tion. The more vulnerable you are, the more people feel the need to protect you." Talking to Margaret, she says, one gets the impression of "a wisdom rooted in intuition, not experience. She is wise in the way that a child is."

Another reporter was traveling in the same car with Margaret during one stretch of the 1974 campaign. He remembers being almost bewitch-ed by her charm. During a half-hour roadside stop, Margaret left the car and ran into an empty field searching for fireflies. The reporter watched her out in the field, completely absorbed and not at all self-conscious, and felt there was an almost magical quality to the scene. He talked at length with her and was much impressed with what she had to say and how she said it—a stream-of-consciousness more than a sustained, thought out conversation. Later, however, he was dis-appointed to find he could not recall anything of significance.

Preparing for the campaign, Margaret had had her hair cut short and bobbed, making her look almost matronly. She dressed to look older and sedate, in demure co-ordinated outfits. After a few weeks, however, she reverted to her usual, comfortable, earth-mother clothes, finally ap-pearing in gingham dresses and Earth Shoes with a lowered heel—commonplace now, but quite unusual in 1974. It was all part of her credo of total honesty, a refusal to compromise.

Having helped her husband win an election, Margaret returned to Ottawa, her home and her family. While things may have seemed rosy on the surface, deep troubles were brewing. Margaret was feeling the strain and responsibilities of her position.

Trudeau and new wife Margaret arrive in Ottawa on March 8, 1971.

ABOVE At Perth Summer Festival, the Trudeaus enjoy a rock band. July 16, 1971.

RIGHT Two years later the somber-looking Trudeaus are seen on Parliament Hill during a Royal Visit. August, 1973.

TOP Baby Sacha in her arms, Margaret and Pierre leave Civic Hospital on December 29, 1973.

BOTTOM Margaret, looking tired, poses with her friend Queen Alia of Jordon at 24 Sussex. August, 1974.

Smoking in public for the first time, Margaret announces she will not be working for Chatelaine magazine. November, 1974.

Pierre's beautiful wife sits on his knee at the Liberal Christmas Party. December, 1975.

Election night, August 8, 1974, at the Chateau Laurier Hotel finds Margaret less than jubilant.

ABOVE During a photo lesson at 24 Sussex the student gets on her knees to photograph Justin. October, 1974.

RIGHT Expecting Michel, Margaret talks with son Sacha. September, 1975.

The Prime Minister's wife dines with Prince Charles. 1975.

Margaret in Liberal T-shirt in Cienfuegos, Cuba, as Castro applauds the Trudeaus. January, 1976.

TOP With her three children (L-R Justin, Michel and Sacha) in tow, Margaret reads a book. September, 1976.

BOTTOM Prior to the official separation announcement, the Trudeaus are seen together on

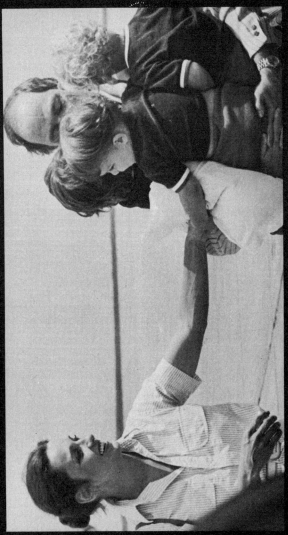

The first picture of the Trudeaus after their separation, as Margaret brought the children to the airport to meet their father. June 16, 1977.

8
Nervous Breakdown

For most Canadians, the first hint of strain in the Trudeau union came in the fall of 1974. Margaret had just observed her twenty-sixth birthday and was well into her fourth year of marriage when the Prime Minister's Office unexpectedly announced, on September 16, that she was in hospital in Montreal for "rest and checkups". Like so many of the announcements about the Prime Minister's wife that had emanated from that office, the notice was carefully contrived and misleading.

Despite the official evasions, news of the hospital stay created a stir across the country. Margaret had already aroused the curiosity of the public with her lively campaigning for her husband in the summer election and, as soon as the official announcement was made, her problems were seen as a result of her sudden unveiling of herself during her spirited campaigning.

In keeping with her disdain for the proper, managed attitude of official Ottawa, Margaret told the truth. She announced candidly that she was being treated for emotional stress. Coming just four years after Tom Eagleton, the American vice-presidential contender, was dumped from George McGovern's Democratic ticket because of allegations that he had been treated by a psychiatrist, Margaret's admission seemed courageous, as indeed it was. She won widespread admiration for her honesty; but with the admiration came permanent celebrity, the everbrightening glare of the public limelight.

The pressures and conflicts that forced Margaret to seek the solace of a hospital bed and the services of a psychiatrist had begun to form during the hard-fought election campaign that her husband had won by a solid majority in July. She had accompanied the Prime Minister during many of his appearances and had been with him when he was booed and when he had strained to use his vaunted charisma to win over voters. Margaret had displayed her own brand of charisma on the hustings, mixing with crowds of Liberal supporters, Trudeau-haters and just plain curious people at political meetings across the country.

In her native British Columbia, Margaret had campaigned alone and effectively. Occasionally, she had introduced herself to reporters covering the Prime Minister's campaign, engaging in often unguarded and freewheeling discussions on the virtues of her husband and the vagaries of life as a mother, wife, and erstwhile flowerchild. She had volunteered to help bring out the votes to keep Trudeau in office, but it had been a strain. He was happy as Prime Minister; she had begun to feel that she would be happy only if he left politics.

During the campaign, there was at least the excitement, the crowds, the television cameras and the headlines to keep her distracted. Perhaps there was a feeling of letdown when it ended. She was bounced back to the constraints of buttoned-up, tight security life at 24 Sussex, and she had probably brought back with her a residue of tension from the constant, grinding pressure of assuming the front-line role of politician's wife.

Her smile, a gleaming ivory Cheshire cat display with which she kept the world at bay, had given way to tears in the weeks after the federal election. Back at 24 Sussex, enclosed in the tight, frightening ring of servants and security men, the fear and the uptight secrecy that is official Ottawa, she thought about herself and the strictures that had made her into a caricature of circumspection. And as she thought about herself, of what she was becoming, she cried.

The sudden end to weeks of criss-crossing Canada in incandescent bursts of publicity left Margaret with the leaden, lonely task of coming to terms with her life. Three years and six months of marriage had equipped her for the roles of wife and mother, in the strictly private sense of relating to one man and the children of their marriage. As she herself put it after her hospital stay: "I needed help because I was really at that time reaching a crisis stage in my life . . . I didn't want to be just caught in the role of politician's wife and I wanted the chance to think about things and to be away from the strains of household and children and just retreat. . . ." She began to feel "very, very weary and very emotionally tight."

Warring within Margaret was the desperate need for help and release and an instinctive revulsion against the stigma that is attached to the mentally ill. Need won out. "I was very, very frightened when I went into the hospital knowing I was . . . now classified emotionally ill, suddenly, because we're not prepared for that." Her knowledge of psychology provided some balance to her fear. In university she had studied Freud and the Freudians and had learned many of their theories. But at school, mental illness had been something in a book, something that happened to other people. In hospital, she was afraid that psychiatric treatment would rob her of something that was uniquely hers. Instead, she found the help she was seeking.

Near the end of her two-week hospital stay, reporters got wind of Margaret's confinement. The public expressed their sympathy by sending several baskets of flowers with cards saying "Best wishes." Public curiosity was expressed by a crowd of about 200 reporters, hospital employees and others who gathered as the Prime Minister paid a visit. Margaret came out of her room, putting on her bravest face before a carnival of television cameras, bright lights, notebooks and microphone cords. "I'm on my way to recovery, thank you," she told the assembly. She smiled and added, "Thank you for all your concern and I hope you'll kindly leave me alone for a while." Her husband, taciturn from the beginning about Margaret's troubles, brushed aside questions, saying, "This is not my press conference, sorry." Later, when she returned home, Trudeau told questioners his wife was doing "just fine" and had returned to her normal routine. That was his last word on the subject.

In 1976, Margaret was universally praised for agreeing to appear in a public service announcement shown on television across Canada to promote Mental Health Week. She had been approached by George Rohn, director of the Canadian Mental Health Association, and had readily consented to appear in the commercial. While the commercial was being filmed at Sussex Drive, Margaret changed the script so that it would express her attitudes about mental health. In the final version, she said: "Mental illness is a real and distressing disease and in most cases it can be treated. One effective treatment is the love and understanding of all concerned . . . the family, the employer and the community. The Canadian Mental Health Association promotes this understanding and help. You can help. Please reach out and contact your branch now."

She also suggested some of the camera angles, and asked that the camera lens zoom in on her face for a close-up when she said, "One effective treatment is the love and understanding of all concerned." In the commercial, she was seen on a living-room sofa at 24 Sussex, wearing a blouse and slacks. In front of her was a freshly cut bouquet of spring flowers, behind her a grand piano. Ross McRae, a vice-president of the advertising agency that had made the commercial, said that because Margaret was interested in photography, she knew where to add the emphasis for her audience. In discussing the project, Margaret had said that from her own experience, she had known that people suffering emotional stress needed not only medical care, but also the love and understanding of people who are close to them.

"She was very open about her former problems," Mr. McRae said, "but when the film was made she was relaxed and radiant. She offered us any room in the residence we wished to shoot in and she couldn't have been nicer."

However, in 1977, plans to have Margaret participate with Rosalynn Carter, wife of the U.S. president, in a joint Canadian-American publicity campaign on behalf of mental health projects were suddenly aborted. An official of the Canadian Mental Health Association said that "Unfortunately, the whole thing has turned sour." The Canadian association was advised that it should forget about arranging a meeting between the two women. "We are not pursuing anything. Mrs. Trudeau has become a very private person." An official of the American organization said the event would not take place "in light of Mrs. Trudeau's current difficulties." Mrs. Carter led a national commission on mental health and discussed her activities with Margaret when the two women met in February, 1977.

When Margaret returned from hospital, the Prime Minister lent her all the support he could. But between them lay the pressures of running the country and a great difference in outlook and temperament. While Margaret tended to respond emotionally, Pierre prided himself on being a rationalist who had subordinated his feelings to his intellect. Most days, their relationship was sandwiched into the ninety minutes or so the Prime Minister set aside for dinner between his hectic daytime responsibilities and the long hours he spent at night attending meetings or reading state papers in preparation for the next day's work. Understating her growing resentment, Margaret said, "It's certainly not the glamorous, exciting life that people think it is."

It wasn't just that she seldom had time alone with her husband. From the beginning of her marriage, Margaret felt the insatiable demands the public often makes upon those thrust into celebrity. In truth, she courted much of the publicity, and in seeking the friendship and guidance of many of the reporters and photographers in Ottawa, she tried to turn celebrity into a controllable commodity: something she could turn off or on like tapwater. Often she succeeded. By granting interviews to a select few reporters, she carefully controlled her image, presenting herself as a loving free spirit who had entered the Prime Minister's residence straight from a west-coast utopia of peace, freedom and tranquillity.

However, she could do little about the heavy-handed security arrangements that government officials felt were necessary to protect her from herself. Although she was occasionally able to escape for quiet jaunts by herself or visits with friends, most of the time she was surrounded by two or more special RCMP agents whenever she left the confines of 24 Sussex. "You just long to walk along and not hear footsteps behind you. I sort of have to look at them as my big brothers, kind of taking care of me. But there are times when you really want to be alone. Lots of times."

She began to envy her friends, young and married like herself, but able to move freely about Ottawa, able to "pick up the kids from nursery school and go down and pick up a quart of milk on the way home or just get in the car and go for a drive and just think things out for themselves." She confided to a national television audience during an interview a month after leaving the Montreal hospital that not having the freedom of her friends was "one of the realities of my life . . . which I find very difficult. It's like being a prisoner because I'm never alone."

At 24 Sussex, the protocol of dealing with domestics was entirely foreign to Margaret, who had grown up in a household full of girls—a household where the work was done by the family with no outside help. Instead of giving orders, Margaret felt sometimes almost as though she should wait on her maids. The servants were uneasy around her, never knowing whether she was going to scream at them or joke with them. Trained to obey orders, they looked to her for direction, and never found it. They responded by trying to run things their own way. "If I say 'No Justin, mother is angry with you, I don't like how you have been behaving,' or 'You know, Justin, you're really being a drag,' he just turns around and goes down to the kitchen and sits on the cook's knee and she's always got cookies for him, and you know, I put strict rules, no cookies for Justin, that sort of thing."

A constant worry was the effect of the tense, unreal atmosphere of the Prime Minister's residence on her children. Having grown up in the 1960s on the easy-going west coast, Margaret was upset by the gun-carrying RCMP agents stationed around the house in Ottawa. What disturbed her more was that Justin, who spent a lot of time talking to and being amused by the Mounties, was developing a fascination with firearms. He'd been told by the agents that their guns were to "shoot rattlesnakes", and with the innocence of childhood, had begun to concoct elaborate schemes and fantasies for dispatching in a blaze of hot lead the swarms of snakes he was convinced imperilled the Prime Minister's residence. Margaret was not amused.

Justin accepted Margaret's illness with a wisdom astonishing in a child of two. "He's been very concerned about me and I have been realistic with him," Margaret said. "I haven't tried to pretend I was off visiting Aunt Bessie in Florida or something. He knew I was in hospital." When Margaret had a quiet talk with him about her illness, he said, "You shouldn't be sad, Mommy, you've got me." The display of solicitude touched Margaret deeply and helped to get her over her depression. "He knew that Mommy was sad and that there were obvious tensions around. But he really helped me out." After Justin's offer to reach out to her, Margaret felt, "That's it, right there, you know. We really aren't alone. We really aren't."

Although Justin appeared to be unusually independent, and his brother, Sacha, was still an infant, too young to be aware of much, Margaret had become concerned about the children. The Trudeaus, mindful of all the attention lavished on the boys by the servants, and their friends and relatives, attempted to take a hard line on treats and discipline. Especially with Justin, the Prime Minister and his wife were "quite, quite strict about not indulging him because he gets too much." But her attempts to correct her son's behavior were constantly being thwarted by the doting, indulgent attitude of others.

Not only were her children and their discipline out of her hands, but the environment in which they were growing up was not entirely to her liking. As she put it herself: "There's this constant threat of violence in our life. I don't want my children growing up in violence. I don't think any mother wants her children to be growing up in an atmosphere of fear."

Perhaps without knowing it Margaret was describing herself as well as her own children. Years after her university days, Margaret still thought of herself as a flowerchild "more than at heart, in my soul". The intimations of violence, the stuffy officialdom, the cloistered sterility of life in the Prime Minister's residence worked on her sensitivities like a canker. She felt like a hothouse flower wilting in an atmosphere too arid and barren to support life.

Still vital was her belief in a universe where people dwelled in perfect harmony—a universe she felt she had grasped during her university days, where there was a "beautiful revolution happening with the flowerchildren or the hippie movement, of getting back to earth."

Margaret's nervous breakdown was a turning point in her life, and perhaps the beginning of the end of her marriage. After she came out of hospital, she became increasingly convinced that she must make a career for herself separate and apart from her role as the Prime Minister's wife and the mother of two children. The election campaign had given her a strong taste of the heady wine of publicity—publicity she felt she was able to control. Out of her stay in the hospital and her return from depression, came a determination to emerge as a woman with a mind of her own and an exciting career that would win people's admiration and allow her to support an

independent lifestyle. At first she believed, perhaps naïvely, that she could pursue a career as
a photojournalist and remain the Prime Minister's wife, trading on her intimacy with famous
and powerful people to receive assignments until
her talent was developed enough to win her jobs
on merit.

The adulation she received as the Prime
Minister's wife often seemed a cruel, empty joke.
It was tantalizing to see her name in the headlines, her face on the television news. But she
realized it was because of the man she married,
not the talents she felt she possessed. In the early
years of her marriage, her dissatisfaction was out-
weighed by the excitement of becoming famous,
and the genuine love she felt for and received
from Pierre. Also, there was the maternal con-
tentment of bright, handsome, developing children. The press, delighted to have a young, beautiful, trendy woman installed at 24 Sussex, made
her into something close to a Canadian princess.

Margaret had entered marriage child-like, and
was never really given the opportunity to become
an adult. Wielding the power and the influence
that she did was pleasant for awhile, but there
were also unpleasant aspects to being the Prime
Minister's wife—playing the gracious hostess,
chatting with a lot of boring older women, endur-
ing the rigid security, and tending her children.
In short, in Margaret's words, it was "a drag".
As the princess began to feel trapped and confined in her court, another regal word sprang to
her mind: abdication.

9

Photography,
Lights, Action!

Sherman Hines is a soft-spoken Nova Scotian who pioneered in Canada a style of photography called "environmental portraiture". Developed in California, it is a reaction to the studied, stilted poses of most portrait photographers. After seeing the formal photographs taken of the Trudeaus, he decided that nobody had captured their essence. His style, he believed, was the most appropriate for the informal Prime Minister and his family.

Early in 1975, he sent a portfolio of twelve photographs to the Prime Minister's Office in Ottawa. When Margaret saw the pictures, she was delighted and invited Hines to come up and try out his style. His photographs of the family at their summer retreat at Harrington Lake intrigued Margaret and she asked him to teach her about photography. A dedicated professional who lectures to his peers in both Canada and

the United States, Hines warned Margaret that if she was considering a career in photography, she would probably be exposed to a great deal of criticism. He added, however, that if she were serious about it, she should get as much instruction as she could before displaying her work publicly.

And so he became her first instructor. "She has talent. I don't know how natural it is," he said. "Some of us have to work very hard at it, but she has enthusiasm, which is probably the most important factor—and most photographers don't have it. She's very enthusiastic and very keen and these are the two criteria that one must have in anything. If she applies them to photography she can't help but be successful."

Hines impressed the Prime Minister as "a gentleman", not at all like many of the press photographers whom Trudeau found brash and rude. When Mr. Hines invited Margaret to come to Halifax to stay with him and his wife and study photography, Trudeau enthusiastically endorsed the idea. In June, 1976, Margaret stayed with the Hines family for about a week. Since then, Hines has kept in touch and his wife has become a good friend of Margaret's.

Hines was teaching Margaret to see "photographs which were uncommon, something out of the ordinary—for instance, a reflection of a reflection, which is a sort of a third-dimensional thing. I was intrigued," he has said, "that she showed interest in that sort of thing." It is too early, he feels, for Margaret's personality to show through her work. "One doesn't put one's personality into one's work for a great deal of time. You don't just immediately start expressing yourself through the camera so you're revealing your soul. It's over a period of time that you develop a style that's your own self-expression. We all try to make personal statements through the lens every time we take a picture, but that isn't something that you start doing immediately, like somebody painting Old-Master paintings immediately, with Old-Master quality. It's not something that you can say, 'Well, that's a Margaret Trudeau picture,' because that's a development. It might take her two or three years to develop a style that would be recognizable and indicative of her personality and of her style."

Hines was not the only professional photographer who helped teach Margaret about the art of photography. In attempting to embark upon a career of photojournalism, she enlisted the help of some of the most talented people in Canada as well as in the United States.

During the 1974 election, a reception was held at 24 Sussex for press people and young Liberal campaigners. It was an informal atmosphere and the guests were all enjoying their drinks when Margaret wandered in and began telling everyone how she'd just taken the children to an Ottawa department store to have their photographs taken for ninety-nine cents. Chatting with Rod MacIvor, a young photographer for United Press International, Margaret revealed her interest in photography and asked MacIvor's boss,

Claude Henault, if it would be possible to take lessons through the UPI office. She received a joking reply in the affirmative, but no one thought she would take up the offer. However, after the election, she got in touch with MacIvor and asked him to begin teaching her black and white photography. They subsequently had a series of meetings beginning in August, 1974, in her sitting room.

MacIvor recalls that on the day of their first meeting she'd had enough of life in the official residence and was isolating herself from the rest of the house, refusing to accept food from the main kitchen and trying not to have much to do with the servants. They sat on cushions on the floor, MacIvor feeling very uncomfortable, being closeted with the Prime Minister's wife under such intimate circumstances. He was greatly relieved when one of Margaret's friends turned up with a picnic hamper and joined them.

After this first discussion, MacIvor began teaching her at irregular intervals, depending on their respective schedules. For the next six months Margaret learned photography from him "more or less from scratch", and in time showed herself to be a photographer of some talent. For example, Margaret took twelve rolls of film during a trip to Europe and not one of them was bad, according to MacIvor.

During one lesson at the UPI office, MacIvor was called out to photograph Governor-General Jules Leger, who was convalescing after an operation. Margaret asked if she could accompany him, saying she wanted to get some real photographic experience, and MacIvor readily consented. Margaret wanted just to tag along as his assistant and remain *incognito* if possible. Garbed in bluejeans, a jean vest, a checked shirt and workboots, she went undetected by an RCMP officer at Government House, the Governor-General's residence. Peter Cowan, then Press Secretary at the House, also did not recognize her. But after she had passed, he suddenly did a double-take. When Margaret explained to him that she wanted to remain undercover, he agreed to go along with the gag. However, she was eventually recognized by other press people during a photo session, and wound up stealing the show from the Governor-General.

The Prime Minister encouraged Margaret to pursue photography, happy that she was developing independent interests. Once, when MacIvor was visiting 24 Sussex for a lesson, he was stopped by the Prime Minister, who asked him if Margaret really had any talent. MacIvor answered, without any hesitation, that yes, indeed, his wife had talent. Trudeau expressed his appreciation to MacIvor for teaching Margaret, and seemed pleased that she was enjoying it so much.

Margaret's initial attempts to become a free-lance writer and photographer were abandoned in a flurry of confusion and embarrassment. In November, 1974, soon after leaving the hospital where she had been treated for emotional stress, Margaret announced that "I have been working on photography and writing and I have a job lined up but I can't say anything about it just yet." A few days later it became known that she had bought an expensive set of cameras and equipment in Europe and was working on a picture-and-story assignment for *Chatelaine*, the women's magazine. However, questioned closely by reporters, she denied ever having said anything about freelancing. "It's all a fabrication," she declared. By the end of November, 1974, she had changed her mind completely and decided to drop all plans to do any writing or photography for magazines.

Doris Anderson, editor of *Chatelaine*, said at the time that she had first been approached by Margaret's secretary, who had said that the Prime Minister's wife wanted to submit some articles and photographs.

When Margaret angrily announced that reports about her discussions with *Chatelaine* were "fabrications", Mrs. Anderson was forced, she said, to confirm that yes, there had been discussions about the possibility of a contribution to the magazine.

"It wasn't so much her fault; it was the press," the magazine editor said. "I don't think she realized what a fuss this was going to make" when she discussed her ambitions with reporters.

Margaret's naïveté seemed to be catching up with her. Nothing was as simple as she wished it to be; with every turn she was faced with reaction, gossip, headlines. Her confusion was becoming a topic of conversation.

Sometimes it must have seemed to Margaret that no matter what she did, the results were disastrous. The press and her husband's political opponents criticized her severely when a newspaper story revealed she had accepted a gift of $2,000 worth of photographic equipment from King Hussein of Jordan in October, 1974.

Canadian laws do not prohibit politicians or their families from accepting such gifts, but officials in the Prime Minister's Office were concerned because similar incidents in the United States had caused a furor in the recent past. One of those incidents had involved a gift by King Faisal of Saudi Arabia of more than $50,000 worth of diamond and emerald jewelry to Pat and Tricia Nixon, wife and daughter of the former U.S. president. In Canada, new guidelines were being drafted about the acceptance of such gifts by Canadian officials because of growing public concern about conflicts of interest.

Also in October, 1974, Margaret was roundly criticized for accepting a ten-day junket to Japan at the expense of Y. K. Pao, a Hong Kong shipping magnate. The trip had cost Mr. Pao somewhere between $20,000 and $30,000. Later it was revealed in the House of Commons that World-Wide Shipping Ltd., of which Mr. Pao was a director and major shareholder, had received more than half-a-million dollars in compensation from the Canadian Wheat Board, a federal-government agency, for delayed grain shipments in 1974. One Conservative Member of Parliament said that even if there was no conflict of interest, the fact that Margaret had accepted the trip from a man whose ships were used by a Canadian government agency gave at least the impression of a conflict of interest.

A total of seven people accompanied Margaret on the trip, including the Prime Minister's brother, Charles, and her sister, Heather. The official reason for the jaunt was the christening of Mr. Pao's new giant tanker, *World Canada*, at the Sumitomo shipyards just outside Tokyo. Margaret's bill for four nights in the Royal Suite of Tokyo's Plaza Okura Hotel was $1,702—or more than $400 per night.

Margaret and her entourage were treated to the most lavish entertainment available in Tokyo, including the Tempura Restaurant, where prices are far beyond the means of the average Japanese. After checking out of the Plaza Okura, Margaret and her party took the famous Japan National Railways Bullet Train to Nagoya City and then to Ise. There, they stayed at the Toba Toba Kokusai Hotel, where the prices ranged as high as $100 a night per person. Later, they went to Kyoto and checked in at the Miyako Hotel, the best and most expensive hotel in the city. First-class air fare to and from Ottawa for the group eventually cost $13,308.

At the christening, Margaret cut the rope revealing the ship's name as about eighty guests looked on and the National Anthems of both Canada and Japan were played. She refused to answer questions from reporters, saying her visit was completely private. Mr. Pao's father pre-

sented her with an expensive brooch at the
christening. Margaret smiled and said only "Gee,
thanks."

Undaunted by the criticism, Margaret has continued to use two cameras for her photography,
one a gift from King Hussein of Jordan, and the
other given to her while she was traveling in
Japan. As time passed, her interest in photography as a career grew. In 1976, after visiting
Latin America with the Prime Minister, Margaret again announced that she intended to con-
tribute to *Chatelaine*. She talked with Mrs.
Anderson about doing a story on day-care in
Venezuela, but it seemed to the editor that
Margaret was unprepared. "She really didn't
have all the information she'd need to do the
story." She suggested that Margaret do some
more research, either by writing to people in
Venezuela or by making another visit. Margaret
planned to make a trip back, but never did.

The assignment was never completed, but in
July, 1976, *Chatelaine* published several pages
of photographs that Margaret had taken of her
family at Harrington Lake. She was paid $800.

Early in 1977, Margaret enrolled in a program
at Algonquin College in Ottawa to learn more
about the technical aspects of photography.
Because she had missed the first semester, she
had to work hard to keep up with the students
who had been in the class since the beginning.
But before she could pull abreast of the rest of
the class, she quit to take a photo assignment
from *People* magazine in New York.

Her instructor at Algonquin, Werner Reitboeck, questioned the wisdom of embarking on a career as a professional photographer when she had had so little experience—not even the technical knowledge to be able to determine what is possible and what is not in an assignment.

"What will happen if the assignment is rough and she gets either no shots or the shots are bad?" he asks, and then answers himself: she leaves herself open to criticism and contempt, because if she continued getting assignments after turning in rotten work, it would seem apparent that she was being used simply because her name sells magazines. For awhile, Reitboeck thinks, she will remain a novelty in photographic circles and continue to sell because of who she is, or was. However, the pressure of assignments will soon expose her lack of expertise and before too long she will be severely disappointed and have to come back down to earth.

Reitboeck thinks that this is a pity, because in his estimation Margaret had the potential to become a good photojournalist. More precisely, he thinks she is "good, but not outstanding".

During the six weeks she was in his class, he liked her because she was a quick learner and an interested student who demanded no special attention. He emphasized, however, that for Margaret, accepting the *People* magazine assignment in hopes of becoming a top photojournalist was just "wishful thinking".

Her presence in the class, Mr. Reitboeck says, did not disrupt the other students; on the contrary, everyone seemed to work harder, was helpful to her and "wanted to look a little better". Reitboeck says that initially he had misgivings about her enrolling in the course because of her responsibilities as the wife of the Prime Minister and the demands placed on her by motherhood. Also, he said, photography has become a romantic pursuit for many people, and he worried because those who romanticize photography often do not take into account the phenomenal amount of hard work that is involved.

However, he said his misgivings proved mostly unjustified and, judging her not as a professional, but as a student, Margaret became particularly adept at documentary work.

For one of her assignments Margaret proposed and completed a series of photographs of a Chinese grocery-store in Ottawa. This involved shooting two or three rolls of black and white film, from which she chose eight shots for a presentation series. "She did a beautiful job." In some ways, he said, she was an ideal student, but he said so with some reservations. For example, according to Reitboeck, a person of Margaret's age and intelligence should be able to resist the temptation to use her privileged position to crash the world of photojournalism. It was obvious from her *People* magazine assignments that Margaret had given in to the temptation. When she attempted to photograph a performance of "Romeo and Juliet" by Canada's National Ballet, she didn't know enough to shoot during those moments when the dancers were almost still. As a result, her photographs were blurred.

Besides these comments, Reitboeck points out that anyone in Margaret's position attempting to establish a career faces certain handicaps. "How many people will tell her honestly whether her stuff is good or bad?" The lack of honest criticism has contributed to her overconfidence and lack of patience in her work, he feels.

During the six weeks she attended the college course, Margaret would arrive every day in her chocolate-colored Volkswagen Rabbit, a gift from the Prime Minister, and take her place in the class like any other student. However, she seemed extremely sensitive to her celebrity, and reacted by trying to make herself as inconspicuous as possible. She asked few questions and contributed little during class discussions. Margaret got along well with the other students, joining them for coffee in the college cafeteria, but in general trying to remain a private person and working very hard. The instructor found Margaret strong-willed and determined, to the point where she oversimplified difficulties that arose. He felt that she wanted to be "Maggie Sinclair, the photographer," instead of "the Prime Minister's wife," and felt that she was in the midst of an identity crisis.

If, indeed, she was going through a crisis, there were those who had no second thoughts about using her anyway. *People* magazine offered Margaret an assignment in April, 1977, and conceded that one of the main reasons for hiring her was the novelty of having the Prime Minister's wife as a photographer. John Dominis, *People*'s photo editor, said Margaret knew how to handle a camera and how to handle people to get them into the mood for a good picture. He suggested, however, that her connections were at least as important as her ability with a camera.

People magazine received enormous amounts of publicity at bargain rates by using Margaret's talents. The weekly—which boasted a circulation of over twelve million—took out advertisements in the *New York Times* in March, 1977, featuring pictures of Margaret and an accompanying text that exploited her position as wife of the Canadian Prime Minister.

Quoting from an article about Margaret that was to appear in *People*, the advertisement read: "Margaret Trudeau walked away from First Lady duties for an 'ultimate freedom trip' to New York where she'd like to be a working photographer. 'Work as a Prime Minister's wife is so boring.'" A picture showed her walking away from the camera in a park in Greenwich Village. She was dressed in tight jeans, high leather boots and a sweater, and her hands were thrust into her back pockets. Another *People* ad in the same issue of the *Times* showed a New-York fireman with his arms around Margaret, who has a camera slung around her neck.

Not only did the freelance assignment for *People* bring dubious credentials to Margaret, but it also got her into further hot water over her use of complimentary travel passes given to her by Air Canada and CP Air. Some Ottawa officials were miffed because the Canadian Transport Commission had turned down an application by Air Canada to provide passes to the wives of cabinet ministers.

Margaret was given the pass as a form of courtesy because of her position as wife of the Prime Minister, and although Trudeau seldom traveled on commercial airlines, using government aircraft instead, Margaret traveled on Air Canada or CP Air to visit her parents in Vancouver. However, when she was traveling between Ottawa and New York in April, 1977, Air Canada asked her to return the pass. "There has been no formal request," an Air Canada spokesman said. "It's just a subtle hint . . . we're not all that concerned about it." When the pass was returned, Margaret was told she would be given free tickets for official trips, but she would have to request them each time. The airline took the position that she should have been using her pass only to accompany the Prime Minister, to meet him or to return from a trip with him.

The wives of great politicians are not expected to have careers of their own, and the established order of things does not include such circumstances. But while there were those who criticized her every step, there were others who stood behind Margaret during her attempts to carve out a career for herself.

Sherman Hines, one of Margaret's first teachers, has remained sympathetic to her throughout the difficulties surrounding her marriage and her profession. The controversy, he feels, "could have been averted if Margaret had the temperament to have a public relations officer that would announce to people where she was going and what she was doing . . . but no one would care, that's no fun. It's just unfortunate, you know, that's the way she runs her life. She takes her chances. . . ."

10
Burying Doctor Spock

Early in 1975, Margaret found herself pregnant with her third child. It was a shock to many people that she could become pregnant so soon after the birth of Sacha and only months after her nervous breakdown. Certainly, there had been great tension in the Trudeaus' marriage and perhaps another child seemed appealing as a way to heal the rifts and soothe the tensions in the union. Or perhaps it was simply Margaret's love for children. Whatever reason she and her husband may have had, Margaret gave birth on Oct. 2, 1975, to Michel Charles-Emile. He was named after the Prime Minister's father, Charles-Emile, who died in 1935.

The birth of Michel coincided, perhaps unfortunately, with Margaret's growing obsession with photography and her designs for independence. When she had visited Venezuela with the Prime Minister early in 1976, about five months

'Try getting away from the
public eye, Margaret. Spend
a few days in New York!'

after Michel was born, she had taken her cameras along and spent hours looking for interesting subjects to photograph. Among the subjects that had captured her attention was the day-care project that she had toured with the wife of Venezuela's president. It was this day-care center that had inspired her attempt to sell a story and series of photographs about it to *Chatelaine* when she returned to Canada.

When her proposal was turned down, Margaret decided to start her own day-care center in the basement of the Prime Minister's residence— or, at least, her version of a day-care center. Certainly it was like no other child-care operation, for it was staffed by the servants at Sussex Drive, with the RCMP security men on duty at the mansion wandering in from time to time to play with the children.

Besides being for her two oldest children, the center was operated for three or four of Margaret's friends from the wealthy Rockcliffe Park area of Ottawa. The existence of the center was not widely known, but word of it inevitably spread around Ottawa. Some cynics suggested that operating a day-care center at Sussex Drive was as pointless and as in poor taste as Tricia Nixon's much-criticized and short-lived program of bringing children from Washington's ghettos to the White House, where she could tutor them in comfort and safety. In all events, the day-care program was also short-lived. After a few months, Margaret lost interest, as she did with so many of her plans during the last desperate year she spent at Sussex Drive.

But her concerns and thoughts about children, mothers, and housewives were to continue over the years.

In mid-1975, while pregnant with Michel Charles-Emile, Margaret had made a headline-grabbing speech defending housewives. Speaking to a gathering of Commonwealth leaders' wives in Kingston, Jamaica, she burst into blazing rhetoric: "Sisters, we must bury Dr. Spock and assert equal rights for women."

Her denunciation of the famous American pediatrician, whose book on child-care had become a bible for a generation of mothers, was by no means an exhortation for women to get out of the nursery and kitchen. In fact, she criticized the women's liberation movement for demeaning housewives. "They downgrade the work that women are doing in the home," she said. "Women should question what they really want out of women's lib."

In a lengthy interview with Judy Morrison of Newsradio before her speech, Margaret outlined her feelings about her role as the Prime Minister's wife, and her thoughts on being a woman.

Q: "Do women in public life have a public responsibility to sort of pave the way even as a leader? Is a woman in that position kind of a pace-setter where women's rights, women's status, is concerned . . . ?"

A: "I think there's a certain element of being in public life (that means) you have a certain amount of power or influence. I prefer to use the word 'influence' rather than 'power', because I don't particularly think that wives have power. I think that we have influence on certain things . . . perhaps as an example to other women of . . . the kind of lifestyle or demands that you make yourself in your own sphere, that can come through public channels—although I don't really believe in the responsibility. I think each woman has a responsibility to determine for herself what she wants out of life and what she's going to ask for, and how she's going to assert herself. . . . The only example that I would like to make to other women is that I stand up for myself. I'm not going to be a spokesman for any particular group or organization, I'm going to be a spokesman for the right of each individual to make her own choice."

Q: "That would, then, be the extent of the limit of your influence or the way in which you would use it?"

A: "Well, I certainly don't feel I have any kind of public responsibility to make speeches and that kind of thing. It's just not part of my attitude towards public life. However, I think there are certain women who can take this stand. I have always felt that . . . it's an individual matter, something that comes from within. The only real measure of it is how much in your own personal relationships, in relationships to the people and to the things and the jobs around you —that relationship is the only thing that counts in the end. I don't think that being honorary chairman of a particular group for International Women's Year really means all that much. You know, what really counts is how you live your life."

Q: "Your discussions will be on the role of women in society. . . . Does the fact that you've never been a career woman . . ."

A: "I was a sociologist for awhile and served with the Department of Immigration and Man-power and I had some different jobs before I was married. I think I'm not a career woman now. I'm not speaking for professional women; in fact, I'm going to make a case for the good old housewife. You know, I think we're being belittled by a lot of ardent feminists. Our job is one which many women feel ashamed of and yet I feel that we are holding a very, very important position in our society and I don't take too kindly to women who suggest that I'm doing nothing because I'm not part of the labor force. I feel that my work that I'm doing at home in raising my children is valuable work and I'd certainly . . . push for housewives being on the Canada Pension Plan and that kind of thing. Because I feel that I work, it's probably more valuable than the work the average woman would get if she went out looking for a job—the kind of work we're doing in the home of raising our children. If we're doing it (and) having respect for the value of family life, the value of raising one's children to grow strong and with clear minds, the value of providing nourishment for our family—I have no shame whatsoever knowing that I'm not working. I don't feel that's necessarily important in order for a woman to be liberated. I think that's part of the free choice that women have to have confidence in themselves in order to make (the choice).

"Now I decided with my husband, I think we made a reciprocal kind of agreement for the first years when our children were young, because of the work that he was involved in and we could obviously see that his work was much more important than any work that I might find for myself during those years, that it was he who would be out working; that it would be me who would be at home. In the future perhaps this will change. Who knows? (Then) I'll be the one who'll go out and fulfill myself outside of the family. He'll be the one who'll take responsibility within the home. I think that you have to have confidence enough in yourself not to be bullied by society. I find there's as much bullying of women to leave their children and go out and work and to find fulfillment. I think that's as much bullying as saying . . . we can't go out and work, we have to stay home and a woman's place is in the home.

"I think a woman has to be able to make a free choice and hopefully she's going to do it with her husband or with the man she's with as partners, sharing the responsibility. If they decide to have children, if they decide their lifestyle involves wanting to have a nice environment, if they want to eat well, if they want to, you know, sort of take these things as important in their lifestyle, then they have to make certain decisions about it. I hate to think that women and men are just doing things in a conditioned way and not thinking about them in a personal kind of way—what's best for each of them, what's best for the man, what's best for the woman, what's best for the two of them together. That's the sort of position that I would push."

Q: "You've mentioned one thing that intrigued me a little. You tended to imply somehow that a lot of the feminists or the feminist notion tends to be a little bit down on housewives and I take it you think of homemaking as a career in itself?"

A: "I think certainly you can. You can get a tremendous amount of satisfaction from being a mother and from taking care of a home and having the freedom of not being committed to a nine-to-five job and being able to work on your own time. I think there's great value in that. Because of our economic situation and the wealth we have in Canada . . . a lot of women are able to not have to be out working. . . . They can enjoy raising their children. I'm very much one for wealth-sharing; I feel this. I found that in studies I've done, that for example, the women of China, who are quite liberated in an economic sense, the women of Russia, different liberated women in the United States who are out working during the day, who are side by side with men, even assuming men's roles such as being engineers and taking labor jobs and so forth. When they come home they're still the ones who have to do the housework; it's not the men who'll do it. They have to carry on two jobs and certainly I think that's one of the real problems that women have to face. (Women are told) 'We need your labor, it'll help our economy, it'll build up our country, we'll have a much stronger labor force if you come in and work.' Tremendous. Then when the suggestion comes that because I'm in there working too perhaps we should talk about sharing the housework and sharing the responsibility of doing the washing and doing the cooking and that kind of thing—the men just say you know, 'no way', so women end up having to do two roles.

"I'm all for men assuming traditionally feminine roles, women assuming traditionally male roles if that's what they want to do and I think it's up to women. Most men are actually quite reasonable, I found, about the subject of women's liberation. They want their women— their women, I shouldn't put it that way—they want women to feel fulfilled and happy and so forth. I don't think there's any man who wants to have a bitter and frustrated wife. I think that they (can be reasonable) when you can make them aware of how conditioned they are in their attitude towards women and make them understand that for the most part, housework is pretty dull and can be pretty repetitive and it's just as tiring for me to do it as it is for you to do it— why don't we share it and the job will be done in half the time and we'll both be free to enjoy each other and the leisure time that we have when we're not working. I think it's a very important point that we have to look at in terms of women's liberation—not just men and their positions but getting men to help us out in roles that have been traditionally defined as women's roles."

Q: "Getting back to the housewife thing just a little bit, you tend to give the impression that working women do not have a good view of the woman who is homemaking. Do you think that the housewife needs to be liberated just a little bit just to gain a little more equality with her working counterpart?"

A: "Well, I wouldn't like to say that all working women put down housewives, but I think I was really talking about the more adamant feminists, certainly the ones who are—who have become very active spokesmen in the women's liberation movement. Some would tend to put it down somewhat but I think, yes, there should be recognition of the value of the work that women are doing in the home. I think it should be an honest appraisal, though. There are some women who really just aren't doing very much and they're not putting very much of themselves into their house, into their raising of their children, because they would rather be out working. Well then, they should appraise it honestly and see that they really are not fulfilling themselves, putting their full potential into the job they're doing and perhaps they should consider getting out and working. There are women who really are dedicating themselves, becoming kind of like professional mothers, professional homemakers, during a certain time in their life. I think it's very important that we women who are being mothers and are in the home get credit where credit's due."

11
A Trip to Venezuela

Pierre Trudeau once said that he had traveled all over the world, but that he was saving South America for his honeymoon. The trip he and Margaret finally took to South America early in 1976 was an official State Visit. As it turned out, it was also more an embarrassment than a honeymoon. As the Prime Minister conferred with government officials in Cuba, Venezuela and Mexico, Margaret, disdaining diplomatic protocol, raised a storm of indignation in Canada.

The most embarrassing occurrence was in Caracas, Venezuela. Attending an official dinner for President and Mrs. Carlos Andres Perez, Margaret decided she would show her admiration for the president's wife by composing and singing a song.

Senora Perez, I would like to thank you. I would like to sing to you.

To sing a song of love.
For I have watched you
With my eyes wide open,
I have watched you with learning eyes.

You are a mother
And your arms are wide open
For your children,
For your people
Mrs. Perez, you are working hard.

The Venezuelan President's wife was so moved by the tribute that she rose, almost in tears, and embraced Margaret. However, Canadian diplomats at the banquet were distinctly uncomfortable and among Venezuelan officials, the reaction was by no means unanimously favorable. Later, Margaret told reporters that Canadian protocol officials had tried to prevent her from singing the song. Apparently searching for a copy of the song, "they tried to take my purse," she said. "Fortunately I had the song in my shawl and there was no problem there."

Another unsettling incident occurred at the beginning of the banquet, when Margaret quarrelled with Robert Murdoch, executive assistant to her husband. As several people listened and watched, Mr. Murdoch walked over to Margaret, who was chatting and shaking hands in a crowd gathered in the lobby outside the banquet room. He remonstrated with her, telling her that she must join the Prime Minister. Margaret complained that Mr. Murdoch was always telling her what to do and would not let her do what she wanted. Then, as she moved towards the banquet room and heard the band strike up "O Canada" for the Prime Minister, she snapped stiffly to attention and gave a mock salute.

Earlier, in Mexico City, she had also ignored protocol by delivering an off-the-cuff speech on women's rights at an official luncheon. It came after her husband and President Luis Echeverria completed an exchange of toasts in the lavish Hacienda de los Morales Restaurant. Her opening observation was that an important international women's conference had been held in Mexico City the year before. "International Women's Year was only a warning that women will take an equal role alongside their men," she said. Then she proposed a toast to Mrs. Echeverria and said she was having a wonderful time in Mexico. Stressing that she was not really involved in the political and economic side of her husband's visit, Margaret added, ". . . but I have learned a great deal about the human side, the spiritual side." Mrs. Echeverria was caught by surprise, and although she had apparently never made a speech at a state function before, was forced to make a reply.

The wife of the Mexican president said she was deeply moved by Margaret's words and described her as a "sensitive, intelligent and excellent person". Observing that she and Mr. Echeverria had paid a State Visit to Canada in 1973, she added, "I had always thought of her as a curious little girl with great big blue eyes. I have seen her grow into an excellent woman and mother. I know how hard it is to be the companion of a man of State." Mexicans, she concluded, love Margaret and "the women of Canada have a great deal to learn from you."

Trudeau, who seemed to feel differently, was seen remonstrating with his wife as they left the luncheon. But the next day at a press conference, he said he had been delighted by her intervention. "When it comes to expressing friendship," the Prime Minister said, "Mexicans probably prefer that to protocol."

In Cuba, Margaret got along famously with Premier Fidel Castro. The gruff, bearded dictator demonstrated that he had a soft spot by taking an immediate liking to Justin. He spent a lot of time playing with the five-year-old, and presented him with a pair of army fatigue pyjamas. One of his gifts to Margaret was a lifetime supply of Cuban cigars, with 200 cigars given to her monthly by the Cuban embassy in Ottawa.

While Margaret thrived in Cuba, the contingent of Canadian reporters and photographers was treated terribly. For about four days, they dined on little but sandwiches and some were horrified when a few of them discovered large cockroaches crawling out from their plates of food. Cuban journalists, on the other hand, were constantly given preferential treatment, to the point where they were even allowed the best seats on a Canadian press truck. Finally, Margaret intervened, and Castro apologized, saying he had to be careful because of the many threats that had been made on his life. Canadian photographers were then given better access for pictures.

While she was on the island, Margaret was presented with a beautiful tortoise-shell fan and an exquisite polished bullhorn necklace. In Mexico and Venezuela she acquired more expensive gifts and consequently spent a lot of time fretting about whether she would have to pay duty on all of the items when she returned to Canada. She did.

When she returned to Ottawa, Margaret was awakened early one morning by a call-in program blaring from her bedside radio. As she listened, she heard callers criticizing her unorthodox conduct in South America. Stung to tears, she called the station, CKOY, and demanded the chance to give her side of the story.

On the air, she explained that members of the Prime Minister's staff were "pushing me very very hard to be on time. Because I was feeding the baby (Michel) and so forth, I was three minutes behind schedule" (for the reception at the Caracas Hilton Hotel). She said a group of vacationing Canadians who weren't "dressed up in fancy clothes . . . real people . . . real Canadians . . ." were waiting in the lobby "and I wanted to say hello to them. I didn't know where our guests were arriving and they pushed me downstairs very very fast."

Margaret continued, explaining that she tried to be "fair about it" because the Canadian tourists had been gathered in the lobby for three or four hours. "I was running downstairs and I started hearing the Anthem so I stopped and the police kept pushing me. I just stopped and stood there waiting while they played the National Anthem." Mr. Murdoch, the executive assistant "apologized to me later when he realized what I was doing."

Denying that she had made a mock salute during the playing of the Anthem, the Prime Minister's wife told the radio audience, "Believe me, I am one of the proudest Canadians there is and I've traveled a lot with my husband and seen a lot of countries and I know that we have a country here which is very special and we're a free people." By insisting on diplomatic protocol, members of the Prime Minister's staff were trying to "make us an élite, and separate us from the people (in the hotel lobby). That is not our way."

As to her behavior, Margaret said, "I was behaving as me. Before I had given the toast and before I had sung the song at this very proper dinner, I had asked if there was entertainment arranged. They hadn't even arranged any Canadian entertainment. So I had written that day a song and I like to sing but my voice isn't very good. It wasn't really a song, it was a letter about Mrs. Perez, who is a woman who is working very hard with the problems of day-care, working in the slums. She took me down to the very poorest slums of Caracas and I was beginning to see the tremendous work she was doing in helping her people. I asked protocol all around if it was all right. I didn't barge in there and do it uninvited. I was invited to do it."

The critical remarks of the radio audience made her feel badly, she added. "When I woke up this morning it was like I felt I should just crawl into bed and not get up and do all the work I had to do because I felt so sad."

Turning momentarily from her distaste for strict protocol, Margaret expressed a strong desire to break away from the confines of her role at 24 Sussex. "I wonder if it's worth it to really try hard to work or whether I should just be a rose in my husband's lapel and should just be a decorative thing or whether I should— because I have received an education in Canada and because I have enough intelligence—be working." She then answered her own question, saying, "I'm not going to be locked away again as I have been in the past and told I'm not allowed to do anything, because I have no rights. I feel that I have. This is a free country which I'm very proud of."

Margaret added that she had been asked to do some work, an apparent reference to the tentative discussion with *Chatelaine* about a story-and-picture assignment. "So I started working very hard and took many, many films, which no press photographer would have been able to get because in some of the countries we visited the military was so hard on the press." She said that on one occasion, "I had ten bruises on my body and a huge scar on my back from the military and the other press pushing me and keeping me away so I couldn't get too close to take pictures. Then they realized who I was and they were very embarrassed and of course let me through and told me I could take all the pictures I wanted and that they wouldn't hurt me." Rather understating the case, she added, "I'm afraid a lot of the Canadian press didn't have that good fortune."

The live radio call, which shocked many people, ended with Margaret saying that she was not as free as she once was "and I'm not walking on the streets as much as I was but I'm going to start."

Later in the day, Margaret attended a tea party for about 500 women whose husbands were attending a conference in Ottawa. She sang the song she had written for Mrs. Perez, sinking to her knees on the plush carpet of the reception room in the External Affairs building when she finished. The Prime Minister's wife received a warm round of applause, and one woman cried, "The song is beautiful, super." During the two hours she spent at the tea party, Margaret was calm and not at all self-conscious. Wearing an embroidered Mexican hopsack dress she had bought during the trip, she smiled as one of the women pinned on it a button reading, "Get Involved with a Grand Old Lady".

The women questioned Margaret closely about the trip, her children, and the problems of being the wife of the Prime Minister. Asked why she had decided to sing the song to Mrs. Perez, she replied, "It's the first time I've been free to sing." She added that she wasn't feeling frustrated with her role; on the contrary, she explained, "I'm feeling free. I've got a lot of stories to tell, and now I'm going to tell them."

Later in the week, she called the radio station back again to answer questions from callers. Aware, however, of the tempting comparison she offered with Martha Mitchell, the eccentric and loquacious wife of the former Attorney-General of the United States, she said the call would probably be her last. As she put it: "I don't want to be Canada's answer to a particular woman down in the States who spent much of her time rapping on the telephone." •

Margaret explained that her role as the Prime Minister's wife meant that people watched her all the time. "I want them to see me as me." She told a caller that she did not think her impromptu speeches, casual dress and spontaneous expression of feelings on the Latin-American trip had affected her husband's image. "When I shine, he shines," she said.

To a caller who said she was upset that Margaret wore jeans, she replied, "I dress and act like a lady most of the time. I have some very beautiful lady clothes." She went on to explain that she had worn jeans during part of the trip because it was convenient and comfortable when she was taking photographs. "Women spend too much time worrying about their dress and too little time worrying about what's coming out of their eyes. It's not how you look but how you are."

Reviewing her marriage, Margaret said, "I didn't have a lot of support because I was not reaching out for it." But she vowed she was ready to "work gently at change", pursuing a career in photojournalism. In answer to one question, she placed herself firmly on the side of women, but indicated that her support for women's lib was less than wholehearted. "Sometimes the women's movement lacks grace and I think women have been blessed with grace."

That night, escorted by an RCMP agent, she saw the American movie about madness and an insane asylum, *One Flew Over the Cuckoo's Nest*. Then she dropped in at the National Press Club and chatted with reporters about the radio program. As she chatted, the Prime Minister's assistant press secretary, Ian Macdonald, phoned her husband, who was across the street in the West Block of the Parliament Buildings planning a special Liberal caucus meeting. The Prime Minister arrived fifteen minutes later and talked informally to the reporters. Then Margaret asked him to dance. They did, for one song, and then left.

A week later, the Prime Minister's Office announced that Margaret had been given a "gift week" in Florida away from her husband and children. Michel, then four months, stayed in Ottawa and Justin and Sacha stayed with their grandparents in Vancouver. In Key Biscayne,

Margaret was the guest of Mr. and Mrs. William Teron, Mr. Teron being president of the Crown-owned Central Mortgage and Housing Corporation.

While in Florida, Margaret retained her growing knack for sparking controversy. Refugees from the Communist regime in Cuba were enraged to read in the *Miami Herald* that the young wife of the Canadian Prime Minister was smoking cigars given her by the Cuban premier. In a candid interview, she said she sometimes enjoyed a cigar with her coffee after dinner. The response from the Cuban exile community in Florida was extreme hostility and she received two assassination threats. When she phoned her husband to tell him, Trudeau was justifiably concerned. He told her that when she returned, "I want you to be smiling as you walk off the plane, not in a coffin." Norman Bouchard, manager of the apartment complex where she was staying, said he was "scared to death" about Margaret's safety. However, she brushed aside the threats, saying the security in the apartment complex was good "and it would only be someone very clever who could really get to me."

The manager's fears were not allayed by Margaret's habit of leaving the complex after dark to ride around alone, on a bicycle. Pursued by reporters on one occasion, she confessed, "People worry about me because they think I'm sick. You can see that I'm healthy." Indeed, with a freshly acquired tan and her relaxed manner, she looked the picture of health.

Margaret was enjoying her holiday, but she observed that Florida was not the place for a country girl. She was right. Seventy per cent of the 600 owners of apartments in the complex were millionaires, and lived a life of tropical, almost vulgar ostentation. She took comfort in watching the sea, "so fantastic and turbulent" and so reminiscent of the view from her grandmother's house in Vancouver. It had been a long time since that peaceful summer.

Margaret felt almost single again, and basked in the relief of not having to "take care of getting my husband off to work at 8 A.M. or deal with three small children as well as the official functions" at 24 Sussex. "I only have to care for myself." She said she had accepted her responsibilities as a wife and mother but added, "It's sure nice not to have to wipe runny noses and mop up after them."

When she returned to Canada, landing at Toronto International Airport, Margaret was again cornered by reporters. She explained that she had "really relaxed and enjoyed myself," but said there were "many people living in the Florida area who are strongly anti-Cuban. They were taking their hate out on me. They almost had a demonstration outside (the Terons' apartment block) but luckily it was called off at the last moment. I can't understand that sort of thing."

Margaret's resolve to emerge as her own person, with her own career, was obviously becoming stronger. However, it was still tempered by love for and loyalty to her husband and children. "I don't want to be a superstar," she told a group of reporters at the airport. "I just want to work. I want to work for the people. I have so much love to give and I want to give it to the people who need it." Explaining her plans to become a photojournalist and freelance writer, she said, "If I can do one small thing, through my words and my pictures which will help someone, I'll be happy."

The differences between her and the Prime Minister were strong, she said, but "we work hard at our marriage because we are such opposites; because I am romantic and he's cool and intellectual." She hoped that "together the combination of us isn't something which he is not pleased by. I think he's a happy man. I hope he's a happy man, because I'm a happy woman, being his wife." The logical, rational mind of her husband did not make her feel inhibited: "I only feel inhibited by dishonest people and my husband is not a dishonest man. I feel inhibited by people who are exploiting and using people for their own gains."

Perhaps it was true that Margaret was a happy woman being Pierre Trudeau's wife. But within a year, she had embarked on a series of activities whose final outcome was her estrangement from him.

'Can you ask Margaret
to ask Mick Jagger
for his autograph?'

12
A Day in the Life of Margaret Trudeau

Margaret's odd behavior during and after the Latin-American trip had left an indelible impression of chaos, confusion and unhappiness on the public. Her denunciations of the restrictions of official life, however, had earned her a measure of sympathy. Her relative youth and the apparent pressures of raising three small children also tended to make people give her the benefit of the doubt. The snippets that appeared in the newspapers and on television about her eccentricity, however, were only the tip of the iceberg.

One morning soon after returning from Latin America, Judy Morrison, an Ottawa reporter for Newsradio, a nationwide news service, spent a day in the disorganized life of Margaret Trudeau.

During the plane ride home from Venezuela, Margaret had decided that she'd like to give a long interview to someone. Back in Ottawa, some of her reporter friends suggested that she bestow this plum on one of the women journalists along on the trip, and Judy was chosen. Well in advance, the two women set 10 A.M. as the time for the interview. When Judy appeared at 24 Sussex at the appointed time, however, she found the mistress of the house still in bed. The interview, Judy recalls, had slipped Margaret's "shake and bake" mind. Ushered into Margaret's bedroom by a servant, she was startled to see four-year-old Justin in the process of ordering his mother's breakfast: coffee and cream of wheat with brown sugar. A maid named Barbara soon brought the meal on a white tray.

Lounging in bed in a long jersey nightdress and a quilted robe, Margaret airily issued orders to the maid without giving her a glance. This seemingly arrogant and rude performance, so much at odds with Margaret's public pronouncements that she treated her servants as friends, set the tone for a distinctly uncomfortable interview. It was startling to hear Margaret, the flowerchild who professed an indifference to things material, curtly ordering the maid to be careful as she set down the tray, lest the hot coffee stain the night table.

One of the problems Margaret had with her servants—and she had many—was that she at first had tried to make friends with them. It was well-intentioned, but it hadn't worked. The servants at the Prime Minister's residence, eight of them, including a nanny, a cook, chief steward and maids, were trained to obey orders. They felt distinctly uncomfortable when their mistress confided in them, quarrelled with them, or sought their advice—in short, treated them as anything but servants. In her early years at Sussex Drive, Margaret was content, by and large, to let the servants run the household with a minimum of interference.

But in the distracted year-and-a-half before she left, Margaret decided to try to take hold. That didn't work either. Again it was well-intentioned. She would announce that there would be a weekly meeting to decide each day's menu, and for awhile there would be meetings. But inevitably, something would come up, an out-of-town trip, a photography lesson, and the meetings would be forgotten. It was confusing, and the servants resented it.

At first she was friendly with all the servants. They were her friends. She had inspirations and wanted to share them with her confidants, the servants. But sometimes it was uncomfortable. Sometimes it seemed like madness.

One of the most memorable occasions—memorable because it was so awkward—was the day Margaret summoned all the servants to hear the good word about relaxing. The word was meditation. She had them all sit on the floor, and told them that they must meditate for ten minutes every day, because it would be good for them. Fortunately for the servants, meditation was soon forgotten.

Servants were rarely dismissed at Sussex Drive. Some of the older ones gradually left, and were replaced with women closer to Margaret's age. But one loyal retainer, a man who had served under Pierre Trudeau's predecessor, Lester Pearson, had had such a violent personality clash with Margaret that he found himself on the receiving end of fits of screaming. After several such episodes, the Prime Minister had reluctantly dismissed him. He had been a good and faithful employee and as a reward for his long service, was given another government job. Margaret sent him a hand-written letter, saying that she had been the cause of his dismissal, and adding apologetically that she hadn't had the courage to fire him herself.

During the six years Margaret was mistress of 24 Sussex Drive, the servants noticed a drastic change in her behavior. At first she was shy but friendly. As she gained confidence, however, she became more outgoing. In the last year, as marital problems and tensions overwhelmed her, Margaret became unpredictable: one day sweet and effusive, the next, cold and withdrawn—or openly hostile. It was unsettling to have to deal with her. Finally, the servants became accustomed to spells of odd behavior on Margaret's part, days when she would withdraw to her own quarters upstairs, cutting herself off from the rest of the house. At any hour of the day or night she might emerge, clad in a nightgown, go to the kitchen, and demand a hotdog or cob of corn, and sit in the corner of the living room by herself, eating silently. For some of the servants, it was a definite relief, a return to normalcy, when the Trudeaus announced that Margaret was leaving for good.

As Margaret finished her breakfast on this particular morning, Judy took in the room and its furnishings. The room was spacious, carpeted in white, and had a window affording a magnificent view of Ottawa's waterways. Margaret lay on a brass bed covered with a white eiderdown quilt and heaped with the day's newspapers. A large table nearby held several books and magazines. The reading material included a copy of *The Joy of Sex*, which had been an international best-seller a few years earlier. Judy noticed several cookbooks as well as magazines like *Redbook* and *Psychology Today*.

In the drawer of her night table, Margaret kept a container full of cigarettes. Throughout the day, she alternated between the cigarettes and an aerosol can of lavender air-freshener which she kept close by. Every time she would finish a cigarette, she'd attempt to banish the lingering smell with lavish use of the aerosol spray. Her husband hated smoking so much, she confessed to Judy, that she had to make every attempt to eliminate traces of her habit before he got home.

By this time, smoking had become such a contentious issue in the household that the Prime Minister had felt compelled to have a "heart to heart talk" about it. He implored Margaret to give up the habit, and Margaret had promised him that she would, as soon as she ran out of the cigarettes that had been given to her during the Latin-American trip. He replied sourly that this would take some time.

Because of Trudeau's feelings on the subject, smoking acquired all of the trappings of an elaborate ritual while she was in the Prime Minister's residence. All of Margaret's ashtrays were kept wrapped in tissue paper and hidden away in cupboards. She and Judy lit up and smoked freely, but it was unnerving for the reporter to have Margaret spraying lavender religiously after every cigarette. At one point Margaret's private telephone rang, and before dashing out of the room, she carefully stubbed out her cigarette. "Rules, rules," she muttered. After returning, she lit a candle so there would be even less trace of smoke when the Prime Minister returned from his office.

After breakfast, Margaret dressed in an adjoining bathroom and took Judy into the upstairs sitting room which she referred to as her "freedom room", apparently because it was a retreat she used when events in other parts of the house became too much for her.

The room had a bay window with the same unobstructed view of the canal as her bedroom. In the bay were two swivel armchairs on pedestals with two electric heaters beside them. A copper-panelled fireplace set into the wall lent extra warmth to the room. It was flanked by built-in, hi-fi speakers for a sound system on which Margaret played albums of folk music throughout the day. The walls were covered in a beige linen material; prominently displayed was a large patchwork wall hanging bearing the Prime Minister's credo: *La raison avant de la passion*. One of the room's odd furnishings was a child-sized cradle decorated like a Ukrainian Easter egg and emblazoned with a hammer-and-sickle. It was filled with large stuffed toys. Around the room were stacks of Canadian newspapers—the *Globe and Mail* and *Le Devoir*. A table was piled high with unopened gifts.

When Margaret finally got down to talking, she revealed that the promise of an interview was just a pretext. What she wanted, she informed Judy, was help in launching her career as a journalist. As she talked, she flipped through an old tattered copy of *Redbook*. She explained that she wanted to write magazine articles and illustrate them with her own photographs. Finally, she turned to an article in *Redbook* on Elizabeth Taylor, entitled "Why I married Richard again," and said that this was the piece that had really fired her imagination.

Incredulous, Judy listened as Margaret announced that she found it impossible to write in anything but poetry, although she considered herself capable of talking in prose. Her plan, she said, was to tape record her thoughts and then hand the tape over to Judy, who would transform it into a magazine article. Her proposed first article was on day-care in Venezuela. Judy gently suggested that North Americans might not find the subject very interesting, but Margaret ignored the hint. Margaret had fixed upon the idea of returning to Venezuela to see Mrs. Perez, this time without all the protocol, to do the research for her article. When she went, she said, she'd take along a lot of information for Venezuelans from the departments of Health and Welfare and External Affairs. She confided to Judy that it was important for Canada to sell its technology to Venezuela so that the balance of trade between the two countries could be equalized. Moreover, she said, she'd enjoyed seeing Mrs. Perez working with the poor of her country.

Having voiced her political opinions, Margaret then held forth on the subject she often kept returning to: her career. Her greatest concern was money. She asked Judy if it would be possible to receive some or all of the payment for a magazine article in advance, and was extremely disappointed when she was told that it was highly unlikely. As to a working arrangement with Judy, she said, with no trace of embarrassment, that since Judy already had a job and was earning a regular salary, getting an interview with the wife of the Prime Minister was remuneration enough. Therefore, Margaret declared, although Judy would do the writing, she (Margaret) would get all the money for any joint magazine articles. Margaret explained that she deserved to get all the proceeds, since she was just breaking into the job market. Later, however, she let it slip that she received half of the Prime Minister's salary to spend on herself, but found that inadequate. In addition, her husband often bought her clothes for formal occasions.

Trying to be reasonable and co-operative, Judy agreed to Margaret's schemes. However, she found it impossible to get Margaret to discuss any concrete plans. Margaret continually turned the conversation back to money. How much could she expect to get per article, she asked. She said at one point that she was concerned about the state of her bank account, but after mulling it over for a few minutes, changed her mind, and said her savings were probably sufficient. One of her preoccupations was her need for equipment to keep her going in photography, including a slide-viewing machine that she expected would cost her a great deal.

After an hour or so, the two women were joined by Diane Lavergne, then the nanny at the Prime Minister's residence, and Marie-Hélène Fox, an employee in the Prime Minister's Office who, on occasion, served as Margaret's press secretary. As the nanny and Miss Fox sat down for coffee, Margaret introduced them to Judy. Afterwards, however, she kept referring to Miss Fox as "Marie-Hélène, my secretary."

Margaret invited Miss Fox to accompany her to Venezuela, on the condition that she pay her own air fare, although promising that other expenses would be taken care of. Miss Fox seemed frustrated and a bit annoyed with Margaret, who kept disparaging any of her suggestions about Margaret's career plans. Seized with the excitement of grand plans, Margaret ordered Miss Fox to have a stock signature prepared for her correspondence, since her career would be taking up most of her time and little would be left for personal replies to letters. From time to time she'd turn to Miss Fox and order her to take notes of the rambling, disjointed observations of the moment. Judy began to have grave misgivings about the project. As it turned out, her apprehensions were justified. After Judy had gone to a lot of trouble to set up a schedule and organize her time so that she could work on the project, Margaret let everything slide. Eventually, the project was abandoned.

Conversing with the three women, Margaret said she was concerned about the controversial call she had made to the Ottawa radio talk show. She confessed that she had made a few errors and wanted to correct them, including the accusation that her purse had been stolen by her husband's aides, when in fact she had forgotten it in a car. She asked Miss Fox to call Martin O'Connell at the radio station and arrange another interview. Reminded that it was O'Connell who had reported her treatment for emotional stress in 1974, she replied that it didn't matter; she didn't care and it had made her feel better to "let it out in the open". Several friends had called to warn her not to talk to anyone or she'd get hurt, but she ignored the advice.

During the day one of her friends called to confirm a luncheon to which she had invited Margaret. In regal tones, Margaret replied, "I would like to receive you here. My chef is really quite good." It was a performance worthy of Cleopatra.

Glancing outside, Margaret commented about the cold February weather. She said that the Canadian people were just as cold, but then changed her mind and said that people who'd called in to the radio station after her outburst had been very sympathetic and supportive of her performance in Venezuela. The winter scene reminded her of an evening she'd once spent at the Chateau Laurier Hotel in Ottawa in the company of Leonard Cohen, the Montreal poet who was the darling of Canadian universities during the early and mid-1960s. Then she mentioned a telephone call from her parents in Vancouver, who were worried about her health. Mr. and Mrs. Sinclair said they had stopped reading newspapers or watching television because her problems had been so often in the news. Margaret said she had reassured her parents and urged them by all means to watch television because the pictures of herself were so pretty. Her other rambling observations included her excitement about a pending trip to Florida, and fretting remarks about what was now an old subject for anyone who knew her well—her lack of freedom in Ottawa. She felt locked up at 24 Sussex and yearned to be free. It was so bad, she said, that she didn't even have her own key to the house.

In the afternoon, baby Michel was put to bed for a nap. Margaret launched into a grand performance, demanding that the intercom in the house be switched on so that she could hear if anything went wrong. However, when the baby

occasionally stirred and woke up, she made no
move to go and do anything about it. Justin and
Sacha had been taken by a servant in the morning to play with some other toddlers. When they
returned, Justin had asked for a spoonful of
white sugar from his mother's bedroom. Margaret flew into a flap, and after a long discussion,
finally decided that he could have brown sugar
instead. Then Margaret washed all the ashtrays
that she and the other women had used, and put
them away, saying "Ha, ha, no trace of smoke
by the time Pierre gets home." Turning to Justin,
she promised him a tea party later in the day.
Then she resumed what amounted to a mono-
logue for the benefit of her guests.

Margaret kept repeating that she needed
healthy people around her and said that she
herself could not function till after ten in the
morning. Although she had many friends and
acquaintances in the Ottawa press gallery, some
of her observations about reporters showed a
measure of contempt and a tendency to manipu-
late and exploit them. She remarked that doing
magazine articles had more appeal for her than
newspaper stories because a magazine just didn't
"go into the garbage" like a newspaper. She said
she would cease giving interviews because journalists were exploiting her as a saleable commodity. "Let the press gallery go mad," she said,
entirely serious. She described British journalism
as "yellow and disgraceful". (If she encountered
reporters while touring around Ottawa on her

bicycle during the summer she had often told them to "fuck off". However, she was just as likely to drop into the National Press Club in Ottawa and chat with any reporters she recognized. Some, including Dan Turner, who now works for the CBC, became confidantes.)

After spending the day with Margaret, Judy came away with an extremely unfavorable impression. She found Margaret overbearing, extremely self-centered and egotistical. Moreover, she seemed completely unable to relax or to concentrate for any length of time. Judy found Margaret's relationship with her servants extremely uneasy and felt that she could not relate well to women. The Prime Minister's wife seemed to have no sense of serenity, no peace of mind. Most of her sentences began with "I", and her conversation was a disjointed stream of associations. She was unsettled and unsettling to watch, seldom able to sit still or keep her mind on one topic. For all her explorations in Eastern mysticism, her preoccupation with meditation, and her denunciation of the grossness of North-American life, Margaret was unable to relax and be her own person.

This, then, was how one woman, who met with and spent a day with Margaret during the winter of 1976—the winter before she separated from her husband—saw her. The public was still largely unaware of her growing dissatisfaction with life at 24 Sussex, but there were many people who had lost their admiration for her.

Margaret was, by this point, a controversial figure; many people resented her, while others heatedly defended her desire to be free.

But no one yet knew how close she was to abandoning her life as the wife of the Prime Minister. That awareness was to come with the spring.

13
The Ultimate
Freedom Trip

The escapade that Margaret was later to describe
as her "ultimate freedom trip" was touched off
by a fight she had had with her husband over
plans they had made to celebrate their sixth
wedding anniversary. Margaret became angry
when Trudeau told her that they'd have to cancel
their plans because of an important meeting. She
decided, on the spur of the moment, to take off.
A few weeks earlier, she'd met several members
of the Rolling Stones rock group in New York
and had been told they would be coming to
Toronto to record a live album of rock music.
Margaret got in touch with a friend in Toronto,
Penny Royce, who works for a film company.
Through her connections in the film and music
world, Penny had learned that the Stones were
staying at Toronto's Harbour Castle Hotel and
would be playing for two nights in the El
Mocambo, a small nightclub.

The Stones had burst upon Toronto on February 28, 1977, amid headlines thundering the arrest of Keith Richard and his common-law wife, Anita Pallenberg, on drug charges. Long before Margaret had left Ottawa to hang out with the Stones, the world knew about the arrests.

With all of the commotion over the Stones in full swing, Margaret was able to slip into Toronto unnoticed, check into a suite of rooms at the Harbour Castle, and carry on as though she were just an ordinary young woman. In an effort to ensure anonymity, she signed her maiden name, Margaret Sinclair, on the hotel register.

Members of the rock group and their large entourage had taken dozens of rooms between the twenty-ninth and thirty-fourth floors of the Harbour Castle, which incidentally, was their second choice as a place to stay in Toronto. Their first choice had been the Windsor Arms, a tiny, posh hotel in midtown Toronto graced with four excellent restaurants and frequented by some of the most famous names in show business. Mick Jagger, the group's dynamic lead singer, had stayed in the Windsor Arms on previous visits to Toronto, but this time the hotel's management regretfully informed him that they were unable to cope with the entire band and its large group of hangers-on, let alone the hundreds of groupies and camp-followers who would flock to the hotel when the word got around.

Margaret arrived on a commercial flight from Ottawa, using the pass that had been granted to her for official trips as the wife of the Prime Minister. She brought with her an array of cameras, films and lenses as well as several suitcases packed with clothes. It was clear she had left 24 Sussex for something more than just a weekend jaunt.

Members of the band had mixed feelings about Margaret's arrival, to say the least. Keith Richard in particular was concerned that word would get around that the Prime Minister's wife had been hanging around, and he feared that perhaps the publicity would interfere with the legal proceedings on his drug charges. The band's advisers and counsellors, who by this time included a high-powered Los Angeles public relations man named Paul Wasserman and a tough, extremely competent lawyer from Little Rock, Arkansas, named Bill Carter, were also worried that the Canadian Government would take a dim view of things. They had no way of knowing if the Prime Minister or other federal-government officials had the power to make things difficult for them.

On the other hand, being followed around by the wife of a Prime Minister is an unusual experience. Anita Pallenberg's first words on being introduced to Margaret were: "Mrs. Prime Minister, you're too fucking much." Wasserman, the wily publicity man, claimed that he did not know how Margaret had found out about the two concerts the Stones eventually gave at the nightclub. He told one reporter that she had met Jagger in February at "Sudden Event", a New York photography exhibit. As the Prime Minister's wife and the rock star chatted while examining photographs, Jagger had told her that the group would be in Toronto the following month.

Since their arrival, the group's greatest concern had been the charges against Richard and Pallenberg. When the rock group had descended from their plane at Toronto International Airport, about twenty miles west of the city, they were met by RCMP agents. Anita Pallenberg's luggage—all twenty-eight pieces of it—had been searched, and she had been charged with possession of heroin and hashish. A day later, Richard had been charged with possession of heroin for the purpose of trafficking, after about an ounce of the drug had been found in one of the six rooms he had rented at the Harbour Castle. When he appeared in provincial court on March 8, 1977, in Toronto, a second charge of possessing cocaine was laid.

The scene in the courtroom that day was almost as wild as a live Stones concert. Hundreds of fans jostled through the corridors of the old City Hall in the heart of the downtown area, hoping to catch a glimpse of Richard or other members of the band. At two in the afternoon, Richard, dressed in a black velvet suit with a gray silk shirt and matching scarf, was whisked through the front doors of the court and up the back stairs. The fans were bitterly disappointed. Some had waited as long as five hours, only to discover that they were barred from the courtroom. Only six reporters were allowed inside.

Richard's court appearance, a routine matter in which he was remanded for a week, took about two minutes. Then he was escorted out, down the back stairs, and through a different exit to the street.

During the court appearance, Wasserman, a tall, obese man who, with his black suit and somber mien, resembled a rotund rabbi, was mistaken by a Toronto radio station for Richard's bodyguard. Wasserman performed many functions for the Stones, chief of which was to keep reporters confused and misdirected. But it irritated him that people would mistake him for a heavy. His job was fending off adverse publicity, not ardent fans. As a flack for perhaps a dozen top British and American rock groups, Wasserman had become a master at misleading reporters. Chet Flippo, an associated editor of *Rolling Stone* magazine who had flown up from New York to do a lengthy story on the Stones' legal problems and live concerts, was told by Wasserman that he had signed up Margaret as a client. "He told me that he was going to represent her, that he was going to be her agent when she brought out a couple of books of poetry. I honestly believed him."

On Friday, March 7, Margaret arrived at the El Mocambo in a rented limousine with Jagger. She stayed with him and the other band members in their dressing room, pouring beer for the musicians and making light conversation until the show started. Then she moved upstairs and sat with a crowd of people that included Richard's lawyer, Bill Carter, Judy Welch, the owner of a Toronto modelling agency, Miss Welch's lawyer, and two of her models. Also at the table, much to Margaret's chagrin, was a plainclothes detective from the Metro Toronto police force.

Along with about 300 other people, Margaret was part of rock history that night in the small, dark nightclub. About a month earlier, Jagger had come to town looking for a place to record a live session for the group's next album. He wanted a club, a place as much like the dirty little dives the Stones had played in years earlier when they had just started out in London. The El Mocambo, a popular little beer joint in the middle of the tatty garment and market district of Toronto, seemed a natural.

For years, the El Mocambo had been a tacky night spot, bedecked with murals of Spanish dancers and easily recognized on Spadina Avenue by an art deco, neon palm tree outside. The club had become one of the underground sensations in the city in 1972 when it was acquired by Michael Baird, a disgruntled businessman who had grown tired of the plastics industry and was seeking a greater challenge for his talents. Baird had turned the place into what he hoped would be a beer joint for students from the University of Toronto campus about half a mile north.

As an opening come-on, he booked a couple of nostalgia acts—Wayne Cochrane and Fats Domino—convinced he'd lose money but hoping he'd attract the heavily beer-drinking university students. The rock-and-beer formula proved an instant success and he had gotten into the business of running what was, in effect, a series of several concerts every week. Sometimes he made a little money on the entertainment, for which he levied a hefty cover charge. And sometimes he lost a little. But he always made money selling beer.

Before the Stones had played the El Mocambo, the entertainment had been a variety of good, but second-string blues and rock bands, mostly imported from the United States. By 1977, however, the club had an enormous following, and on any night when even a moderately well-known group was booked, it was difficult to get a seat.

The main room upstairs at the El Mocambo is a dreary dungeon of a place, a monument to the secret shame that having a glass of beer used to be a decade or two ago. Catering to a crowd of students and other assorted music lovers oblivious to the decor, Baird made no attempt to brighten up the place. "We didn't have any idea of making it a rock place at all. I'd never even heard of ninety per cent of the acts that we wound up booking." The El Mocambo crowd became a most enthusiastic collection of people —few of them older than thirty—who came to pick up dates, listen to good music, and drink beer from outsize bottles. In short, they were exactly the sort of audience, and the El Mocambo exactly the setting that Jagger was seeking for his live recording session.

Baird knew about the planned recording

sessions weeks in advance. As the actual week arrived, though, he wasn't at all sure that it would come off as planned. "All kinds of things go through your head. It was supposed to be Tuesday, and that was cancelled. Then Thursday, and that was cancelled. So you end up saying to yourself, 'Well, I'll believe it when I see it.' " The audience for the recording session was selected, deviously, by Toronto's largest rock music station, CHUM. Two contests were run by the station, one for AM listeners and the other for the FM audience. CHUM-FM listeners were asked to write why they would want to go to a party with the Rolling Stones. AM listeners were asked to pick up tickets for a live recording of April Wine, the warm-up group when the Stones actually appeared at the club. The El Mocambo announced that it was closed for repairs, and recording equipment was secretly brought into the building.

Respondents to both radio contests were asked to meet at CHUM at six on the night of the Friday session, where they were put on three chartered buses. As they boarded the buses, they were told what they had really won: they were about to hear the Stones live at the smallest club they had played in in years. The buses proceeded to a subway station where they were unloaded and all passengers were searched for cameras and tape recorders and asked to identify themselves. By this time, the rumors had spread that the Stones were to appear at the club, and police had thrown a cordon around the building to keep away hundreds of curious fans. The buses moved through the police lines in the alley behind the club and the passengers were searched a second time before being admitted through the rear exit. Reporters were let through about two hours later.

When April Wine had finished playing, the Stones and Margaret came up from their dressing room and the crowd went wild. As the band swung into their first song, "Route 66", people were dancing on their chairs and tables, spilling gallons of beer, clapping and cheering. Margaret and her group were seated well back from the band at first, but one of the Stones' entourage interceded and they were moved up to a table almost at ringside. One of the models accompanying agency owner Judy Welch bore a remarkable resemblance to Jagger's wife, Bianca, and was besieged by autograph seekers. When Margaret noticed the swarm around the woman, she turned and asked, "What's happening?" The model calmly stopped signing phony autographs for a moment and explained. Margaret seemed mildly amused, but soon turned back to the music. Other people at the table thought she seemed relaxed, intent only on enjoying herself. With the Stones blaring out heavy rock, it was almost impossible to make conversation, and although a few of her table-mates tried to chat with her, Margaret kept very much to herself. No one in the audience seemed to recognize her, until a man sitting in front of her said to his wife, "That's Margaret Trudeau." The wife looked intently at her, nodded, and then turned her head. It turned out that the man was the chauffeur for the band: Margaret had escaped recognition outside the Stones' entourage.

The Stones played for two hours a loud recapping of many of their hits—"Let's Spend the Night Together", "Little Red Rooster", "It's Only Rock and Roll", "Jumpin' Jack Flash". At the end of the night, the band returned downstairs and Margaret went with them. A small party was held for about twenty-five people—club employees and a few other select people. It was a quiet affair, and Margaret stayed close to the Stones, who huddled in one end of the room, trying to stay away from the other people. After about an hour and a half, the party broke up and the band returned to their hotel. Margaret rode with them. Later, in the hotel, Chet Flippo, the *Rolling Stone* writer, observed Margaret, "in a white bathrobe wafting down a corridor".

By Saturday, the press had caught on that Margaret was in town. Primed by her bizarre performances in South America and rambling calls to the Ottawa radio program, the Toronto newspapers were eager to find out what she was up to. Word sifted through that she had been at the Stones concert the night before, and the fevered prose about the Stones contained references to the Prime Minister's wife being in the audience. As Flippo noted in his *Rolling Stone* story, "None of the Toronto papers know that she is at the hotel, despite the fact that the Toronto *Star* offices are just across the street."

However, people began seeing Margaret in the

hotel lobby, browsing around the newstand, and the hunt was on. Despite the Stones' reservations about her presence, she was given free run of their suite on the thirty-fourth floor. While the musicians relaxed watching television or making idle chatter, Margaret was often with them, affecting a nonchalance, smoking cigarettes, occasionally drifting back to her own suite to make telephone calls. On Saturday afternoon, Jagger summoned Flippo to the suite. Margaret wasn't around. Flippo asked Jagger about the Prime Minister's wife, and Jagger replied: "She just dropped by. Someone said she wanted to come to the gig, so we took her. I had never met her before. But I guess she likes to go out to clubs and go rocking and rolling like everyone else—young girl, you know." Charlie Watts, the Stones' drummer, who had been listening, added: "One of our mums." That's about as explicit as the Stones got about their new fan.

That night, Saturday, there was a second recording session at the El Mocambo. It was an abbreviated version of Friday's performance, but the fans, again hand-picked by CHUM, were just as uninhibited in their rapture for the Stones.

Margaret was sitting ringside again, but this time she'd brought her camera. She and the Stones' own photographer were the only people in the place allowed to take pictures. Flippo wrote: "Jagger, in a little green and white striped jumpsuit open to the point where his pubic hair presumably begins, put on the most defiant, cocksure, strutting performance I have ever seen.

The band members sign autographs in between numbers and at one point Jagger ends up on his back with a female admirer lying on top of him, kissing and feeling." Margaret energetically snapped pictures through the whole performance.

A party was arranged after the performance at the posh townhouse of Judy Welch. CHUM had rented the house for the evening and about 200 people were invited. Hundreds of others learned about it from whispers around the El Mocambo, but the Stones threw most potential party-crashers off the track by heading to the Harbour Castle in their limousine, and then slipping out a back door. Miss Welch personally extended an invitation to Margaret, who begged off, saying she had a prior engagement. "Perhaps she was afraid to go because it was at a private home," Miss Welch said. No one knows, or no one is willing to say, how and where Margaret spent that night.

The party at the model agency owner's house began at ten but the Stones didn't arrive until after midnight. As soon as Jagger entered the room he was mobbed by about a dozen young women. Miss Welch said later: "I invited a lot of good-looking girls just to provide some pretty faces. I didn't think they'd react the way they did. A lot of them had steady boyfriends, but not one of them wouldn't have gone to bed with Mick that night." One woman, at least four inches taller than Jagger, made a beeline for him and, according to an employee of Miss Welch, "in two seconds she had her hands down his pants. It was just amazing to watch. Mick seemed to like her, though. He seemed to be enjoying the whole thing." With the drug charges pending, Miss Welch said, "No one was using anything. I didn't notice anybody even smoking grass." However, the radio station had been generous in laying in stocks of liquor and wine and most of the guests became noticeably drunk. "Everything considered, it went well. Everybody behaved themselves," Miss Welch said. The only disruption during the long night came when the manager of the radio station was punched in the face and knocked to the ground by an irate member of April Wine. The party broke up at about seven in the morning when the Stones departed to have breakfast at the elegant Courtyard Café in the Windsor Arms Hotel. After a leisurely breakfast, they returned to the Harbour Castle to sleep until early afternoon.

Miss Welch was invited to the Stones' suite the next day and gladly accepted. She arrived at the thirty-fourth floor of the Harbour Castle at about 2 P.M. and members of the band were drinking wine and watching television: a perennial pastime, it seems, of touring musicians.

Margaret strolled in a couple of hours later and champagne was ordered in her honor. She sat on the edge of Jagger's bed sipping at a glass. Keith Richard's seven-year-old son, Marlon, was playing on the floor. Margaret knelt down and began talking with him, and during the next few hours, helped him as he drew pictures and toyed with a coloring book and crayons. Marlon

seemed to accept her as his friend, and it was
obvious from their conversation later that they
had spent a great deal of time together while
Margaret was at the hotel. Once in awhile she
joined in the conversation of the adults, lit a
cigarette or sipped at her champagne, but mostly
she played with Marlon. She did not mention her
own children back in Ottawa with their father
and the servants. When a hockey game came on
the television set, Margaret settled back to watch
it with the others. She rooted for the Montreal
Canadiens.

When Margaret left later that evening, someone expressed concern about her walking the
halls alone. There were dozens of fans desper-
ately trying to get near the Stones, and some of
them were probably unbalanced, if not dangerous. However, Peter Rudge, the Stones' manager,
said in the hotel room that night that Margaret
could look after herself, and mentioned that she
rode unmolested up and down the elevators all
the time without an escort. By this time, a crowd
of reporters had descended on the hotel, trying
to find out where Margaret was staying and what
she was up to. The hotel management and
employees insisted right up to the minute she left
that the Prime Minister's wife was not registered
at the Harbour Castle. Realizing that the press
was in hot pursuit, Margaret kept very much to
herself. In fact, most of the time she had spent
in her room writing letters or watching television.

On Tuesday, March 8, Margaret packed up
her luggage, assembled her camera equipment,

descended to the lobby of the Harbour Castle, and at 1 P.M., checked out. She met Paul Wasserman, the public relations man, and told him she was headed for New York City and would be staying there until March 17, when she had to return to Ottawa for a public appearance. By that time, Jagger and guitarist Ron Wood had headed for Manhattan on separate flights. During the late afternoon, reporters and photographers from the three Toronto papers staked out the hotel's lobby, desperate to see and speak to Margaret. Wasserman, ever the consummate manipulator, feigned ignorance for hours. He had been enjoying every minute of what was to him, a unique situation. Finally, after several martinis, he confided to a reporter that Margaret had left for New York. He said Jagger and Wood had also left that afternoon, but couldn't say if they went on the same flight. Jagger, he said, had gone down to visit his daughter, who was staying with her mother in a townhouse that Jagger had recently bought in Manhattan. Wood was just fed up with all the publicity, and wanted to take a break from everything.

The story of Margaret's departure made the final editions of the next morning's *Globe and Mail*. The newspaper also reported that an official in the Prime Minister's office did not know whether Margaret was still in Toronto or when she would return to Ottawa, ". . . but we take the position that since she was not on official business, it is none of our business. We're trying to find out ourselves where she is." After hedging on the first of a barrage of queries from reporters about Margaret's whereabouts, the Prime Minister's aides singed the telephone wires in the nation's capital as they tried to co-ordinate their responses with each other. The confusion was finally handled by an attempt to stonewall reporters' queries on the basis that since Margaret's Toronto trip had been made in a "personal capacity", it was not a legitimate concern of reporters.

Well ahead of time, Margaret had arranged to stay in New York at the luxurious Central Park West apartment of Yasmin Aly Khan, daughter of actress Rita Hayworth and the late Aly Khan. Margaret and the Prime Minister had met Yasmin on a yachting trip a few years earlier.

Back in Toronto, Wasserman, despite a late evening of heavy drinking, had risen early and picked up copies of the morning papers. Seeing the front-page *Globe* story saying that Margaret, Jagger and Wood had all departed for New York, he phoned *Rolling Stone* writer Flippo in a state of extreme agitation. After reading an editorial in the *Sun,* saying "C'mon Maggie, either behave with distinction or stay at home," he decided it was time he left Canada.

Later that day, safe in his New-York office, Wasserman said the newspaper story claiming that Margaret had planned to accompany Jagger and Wood to New York was the result of a misunderstanding. "Mick went on a 5:30 plane and Ron Wood and Peter Rudge left on an 8:45 flight. They say she wasn't on either flight." He said he "might well have misled" the reporter. "I was under terrible pressure yesterday. It may well have been my fault." Aides in the Prime Minister's Office were saying only that Trudeau was well aware of his wife's whereabouts "but we are not confirming or denying any details of her trip."

Margaret had become an international personality. Toronto newspapers received telephone calls from the B.B.C. in London and a radio station in Melbourne, Australia, inquiring about the Prime Minister's elusive wife. In Toronto, CHUM was offering $500 to anyone who could disclose Margaret's whereabouts.

Meanwhile in Manhattan, Margaret busily set out to arrange a schedule that combined both business and pleasure. The pleasure included an evening at the ballet with Yasmin Khan, followed by a quick tour of some of the city's fashionable drinking and dancing spots. With Yasmin, she appeared at the City Center Theater wearing a dark mink coat over a burgundy red silk-on-silk dress, in sharp contrast to the casual clothes she'd affected while wandering around with the Stones in Toronto. Questioned by reporters in New York, she denied going into hiding. Asked about Jagger, she said, "I'm fond of him and would like to think he's a friend. But I hardly know him." Jagger issued a statement saying, "Really, this whole thing is ridiculous. Margaret Trudeau is a very attractive and nice person, but . . . I never met her before and

I haven't seen her since I got to New York. In fact, I have not seen her since Sunday."

After the ballet, a benefit performance for the Eliot Feld company, the headline-catching Margaret went to Regine's, one of the most fashionable discotheques in town. For the ordinary customer, the cover charge is $10 a head, plus a large bribe for the doorman. Two Canadian reporters trailing Margaret had to pay $60 to get seats and were charged another $37.50 for four small glasses of mediocre white wine. They missed Margaret and Yasmin Khan, who had been tipped off by an employee and smuggled out before the press could get to them.

The next day, Thursday, Margaret had arranged to visit the studio of New-York fashion photographer Richard Avedon, who has won an international reputation for his work. One of Margaret's close associates in Ottawa said that she had departed for New York in the expectation of working alongside the master. The New-York tabloids, the *News* and the *Post,* contained sensational and highly speculative stories about Margaret's whereabouts and activities. In London, the British popular papers had cleverly managed to link the words Margaret, Stones, and Scandal, in most of their banner headlines. The *New York Times* ran a short, restrained story in its back pages, noting only that the Prime Minister's wife had scheduled an appointment with Avedon.

Early Thursday morning, reporters began to

appear at the photographer's studio on East Seventy-fifth Street. They were informed that they were on a wild-goose chase; the studio knew nothing about Margaret Trudeau and she would definitely not be anywhere in the area. Several of the earlybirds in the press corps accepted this and took off. By 11 A.M., two Canadian reporters had staked out the studios and were determined to wait for her all day if necessary. They were soon joined by another pair of Canadian reporters, and then by a United Press International photographer, a couple of freelance photographers, a few more wire-service people and finally, by three Fleet Street reporters eager to dig up the dirt for their respective British dailies. Soon, word spread that Margaret was to appear at 12:30 P.M. The time seemed logical, since at least half of the reporters were aware that the Prime Minister's wife rarely got out of bed before eleven. Horror stories were quickly exchanged among the reporters about the search for Margaret, and then everyone settled down to wait for her. It was a bright, warm day, a stroke of good fortune for most of the Canadians, who had been dispatched to New York with no time to collect overcoats.

Finally, Margaret arrived in a taxicab. She fumbled in her purse for change, and as she did so, the vehicle was surrounded by photographers. Realizing that he had a celebrity for a fare, the driver accepted payment, and then pushed a piece of paper towards her. Margaret signed the autograph for him and then quickly alighted

from the cab, smiling, greeting a couple of
Ottawa reporters by name, and making her way
slowly into the studio. Questions were shouted
at her, but most of her replies were inaudible.
However, asked if she were having an affair
with Ron Wood or Mick Jagger, she replied,
"Certainly not." The doors closed behind her,
and the journalists settled down for another
long wait.

With Margaret secure behind the heavy
wooden doors of the studio, the press began to
map out strategies to ensure that they would be
able to interview her when she came out. Tours
had already been made of the area and as far
as anyone could determine, there was no rear
exit. It was impossible to be certain, however,
because in the rabbit warren of buildings in
midtown Manhattan, there are often fire escapes
on rooftops, or passages through basements.
The British reporters began to swap stories of
other famous manhunts they'd been on, and
one recalled how the Beatles, at the height of
their fame, had once escaped a flock of reporters by riding off in an ambulance. After that
anecdote, heads turned anxiously every time an
ambulance went down the street, which averaged
about once every half-hour because of a hospital on the next block.

The three British reporters, all armed with
pocket-sized tape recorders, and obviously accustomed to working as a team, went into a
huddle to plan how they would handle the situation. After a lot of talk and laughter, scrib-

bling of a few marks in their notebooks for show, and phone calls to their respective offices, two of them took off to dine at a restaurant and bar on the corner, leaving the third to alert them if Margaret came out early. The Canadian and American reporters, unaccustomed to collaborating with competitors, were at a decided disadvantage. They grimly stood watch on the sidewalk, venturing away from the site only to use a pay phone a couple of hundred feet up the street, or to a restaurant to quickly use the facilities when the call of Nature overcame their fear of missing Margaret. No one wanted to be remembered as the reporter who pissed away the story of the year.

When boredom set in, a reporter and photographer organized a game of chance, tossing dimes to see who could come closest to the side of the photography-studio wall. The building and the sidewalk had some interesting curves, and it was a diverting game for the onlookers. From time to time, studio employees would emerge to offer words of encouragement like, "Why don't you all go away?" or "Goddamned paparazzi," or "You must be kidding!"

The eldest of the three Fleet Streeters, a tall, middle-aged man in a heavy overcoat, decided to show a little enterprise. Getting to his knees on the sidewalk in front of the studio door, he lifted the metal flap of the mail slot and peered inside. A colleague standing beside him addressed the bald spot at the back of the peeper's head. "Right. Give us a running commentary.

Tell us what's going on in there." The peeper obliged. "I see lights. I see bright lights, strobe lights, I think. There's a photo session on." Suddenly, he tensed and said, "Ah, fuck. Someone is coming." The letter slot clattered shut as he bolted upright and away from the door. A loud chorus of laughter erupted from the journalists watching him; the afternoon sun shone brightly on this performance. Behind the mail slot, Margaret was chatting happily with Avedon and his assistants, a male fashion model, and an actress from a television soap opera. Avedon was taking photographs for a Revlon cosmetics advertisement. As the peeper from Fleet Street had been discouraged from embarking on a career of keyhole surveillance, he recruited a twelve-year-old boy to do the job for him. The boy obliged with a stream of gibberish about how many legs he could see and speculation about whether they belonged to men or women.

Next a limousine pulled up about 5 P.M. and reporters rushed to line up taxicabs to follow it. The limousine driver patiently answered questions about his intended passenger, the actress. A frizzy-haired woman then came out of the studio and the Fleet-Street peeper, his deadline upon him, was after her, believing that she was Margaret disguised in a wig. Striding alongside her, he asked why she had cancelled an appearance in Nova Scotia. The woman, though, had never heard of Nova Scotia.

Finally, at 6:45, as the light on the street was

failing, Margaret came out. She smiled to her audience and asked reporters, "Are you still here?" Chatting with the reporters nearest her, she signed an autograph and entered the limousine. Three taxicabs followed bumper-to-bumper and Margaret was delivered to Yasmin Khan's apartment building about two miles away. As soon as the limousine had stopped, the mail-slot man was upon her. Flinging his arm around Margaret, to the horror of Canadian reporters, he peppered her with questions about her relationship with the Prime Minister. By this time, Margaret had already made up her mind to seek a separation and make a living as a photographer in Manhattan. In fact, she'd called Trudeau from New York and told him about her plans. But she still wasn't ready to say anything about it in public. The Prime Minister's Office had issued another of its evasive statements, saying that Margaret was cancelling all her appearances due to "unforeseen personal circumstances". Pressed on this point, Margaret said: "What unforeseen circumstances?" She stated that she had cancelled the appearances herself for "the time being".

As to why she was cancelling her commitments, she said, "I'm tired of the public." Surrounded by reporters and photographers as she walked into the lobby of Yasmin's apartment building, Margaret said she wanted the press to leave her alone. Then she added, enigmatically, "After six years of this, I've had enough." Asked about the state of her marriage, she replied: "I feel fantastic." Then she got into the elevator and disappeared. A reporter who called later was told that Margaret intended to spend the evening watching television.

The rumors of trouble at 24 Sussex were fanned by Margaret's declarations. When word began to spread that she had shopped around New York for photography assignments and was working on a freelance job for *People* magazine, the assumption became general among many observers that a separation was inevitable. John Dominis, photo editor of *People*, first became aware of Margaret after he'd sent a reporter-photographer team to Ottawa to do a spread on the Trudeaus. The photographer looked at Margaret's pictures and took a few back to New York. Dominis was particularly impressed with a shot she'd taken of Yasmin sticking her head out of a window of her apartment. "It was a very good—an unusual glimpse of New York." When he found out that the Prime Minister's wife was anxious to break into photojournalism, he had New York photographer Oscar Abolafia bring her in to him. Their first meeting was immediately after the partying in Toronto with the Stones. If she had not been the Prime Minister's wife and hadn't been introduced by Abolafia, Dominis says, he would not have considered giving her an assignment. She impressed him, though, with her enthusiasm, and he asked her to take pictures of Duane Bobick, the heavyweight boxer trumpeted at the time as the sport's latest Great White Hope.

Realizing Margaret's publicity potential, Dominis assigned Robin Leach, a British freelance writer, to accompany her and Abolafia around New York while she took pictures. Leach turned in a story that became a greater scandal than Margaret's trip with the Stones. She was quoted as saying that both she and Trudeau "gave up our lovers when we married". The article contained details about the most intimate aspects of the couple's married life. For example: "Pierre loves me to be good looking and he's my number one fan—he has the body of a twenty-five-year-old, and what pleases him, pleases me. I don't have a single sheer negligée, but I'll normally wear a garter belt and stockings. I like putting them on. It's a turn-on."

Responding to criticism of the calf-length dress she had worn at a White House dinner in February, she said: "Pierre said I should wear it. He used to not like me wearing my sexy clothes, but not anymore. If I don't feel like wearing a bra, I don't wear one. I'd never let my nipples show at a state occasion though— I'd be frightened the old men would have heart attacks."

Margaret confessed to having "strong sexual energies". At that point, she was still denying rumors of a separation. "I'll commute to Ottawa, so I can still be Pierre Trudeau's wife and the mother of our three children . . . but I also want to be a working photographer." Accompanying the article were some examples of her work, including shots of Yasmin and Jagger, and some scenes in Greenwich Village.

She continued: "I pray that people will not judge Pierre by my wanting to be a woman. But I am a free spirit that must survive in a free world. I am not a weirdo, a wacko or an eccentric for wanting to do good, honest work on a day-to-day basis. I just want to find my individuality."

By this point, Margaret was the most talked-about woman in North America, if not all of the English-speaking world. For a woman who did not want any publicity, she was having an incredible effect. Many Canadians felt by now that she was a frivolous, confused, selfish and glamour-seeking young woman. Others, however, still vehemently defended her right to do what she wanted to do, and to go where she wanted to go without interference by the press.

It has been surmised by some that Margaret, although she claimed that she wanted to be left alone, was actually seeking to be a celebrity. In fact, the news coverage she received during her "ultimate freedom trip" was much greater than any she had previously had while on the election trail with Pierre. And this time, all of the publicity was directed towards her alone. Some people have even gone so far as to say that she was jealous of Pierre's attention and tried to embarrass him in public to get back at him for leaving her on her own so much of the time.

But whether or not she really did want to be alone, Margaret was pursued everywhere she went. The public was as always curious to know what was happening to the Prime Minister's wife—the woman who, only six years before, had been the darling of the Canadian people. They wanted answers to their questions: Why did Margaret feel so constrained by her life that she would allow herself to create a scandal in order to show her discontent?; Who was the "real" Margaret Trudeau?; And most of all, what would she do next?

And in the days that followed, Margaret gave the public even more to discuss, to argue about, and to accept. Although ultimately, she did not answer the questions that were on so many minds, she did finally make public the depth of her discontent.

'Poor Pierre. He hasn't been the same since his wife left him.'

14
Pierre Elliott Trudeau

On the evening before the announcement of his formal separation, the Prime Minister attended a going-away party in Ottawa for a member of his staff. He arrived alone and seemed to be in good spirits. During the few hours he was at the party, Trudeau made small talk with several people and even joked a bit. People who worked with him daily said he had not looked so relaxed in months.

Possessed of an obsession about his privacy and the sanctity of his family life, as well as an almost old-world sense of chivalry about women, Trudeau had never uttered a word of criticism in public about Margaret's conduct during their marriage. While he never really felt he had to apologize for her, the Prime Minister occasionally did offer explanations and spirited defenses of her more bizarre performances.

Soon after the separation, he worked long into

the night at his office with some of his colleagues. When he left, he invited one of his associates back to 24 Sussex for a late-night snack. Together, they examined the huge, walk-in freezer that supplies the kitchen at the Prime Minister's residence. The freezer contained only two frozen pork chops. Trudeau remarked sadly, "Well, I guess we haven't kept the inventory up." A few days later, he had lunch with two of his staff members. Always a fastidious eater who, during his marriage, seemed to have dined mostly on health foods, Trudeau ordered calves' brains. He remarked that with Margaret gone, he could at least eat whatever he pleased.

The Trudeaus' marriage had been punctuated by Margaret's periodic public complaints about her loss of freedom, her feeling of confinement, and her need to express herself in her own terms. While it is true that Margaret's freedom was often curtailed by the life she had married into, it is also apparent that Trudeau himself must have often felt cramped and hemmed in by the life he had chosen. By all accounts a compulsive worker who labors long hours in his office five days a week, the Prime Minister is also a devoted father who has seized every opportunity to spend time with his children. Margaret seemed to be constitutionally incapable of rising early in the morning, and it was a rare day that she made it out of bed before eleven. Trudeau was usually up hours earlier and, during the last years of their marriage, would have breakfast with his two sons every morning before leaving for his office. Although Margaret declaimed often on the subject of children, it seems to have been the Prime Minister who was the more devoted parent.

In 1975, in an interview recorded in London by the B.B.C., the Prime Minister had given a rare public account of his feelings about married life. He was interviewed by Lord Chalfont, a writer and broadcaster who from 1964 to 1970 was Minister of State in the government of Harold Wilson. Lord Chalfont asked the Prime Minister if having married a very beautiful woman considerably younger than himself had affected his attitude to life and to people. Trudeau had replied that he thought it had. "I think it is important for a parent to minimize the distances between himself and his children, and it's probably important for a political leader to minimize that difference." Trudeau said fast-changing modern values can cause a generation gap within six years. "For all these reasons I felt it important for me as a family man to not be too far away from my children. I hope I am young enough in spirit and I wanted to be closer to my children, which is obviously easier if you have a young wife than an older one. Same thing in politics. I think in that sense my wife helped me to understand new values, what interests the young people today. When I married her, she had only been out of university a couple of years: I was able to listen to her and understand what their worries were, what their aspirations and ideals were."

Lord Chalfont then asked Trudeau if marrying

a prime minister had not created pressures for Margaret. He admitted that the pressures were considerable. "I confess that like most husbands, I suppose I didn't realize how great they were. You know, marriage can be a regressive institution. Oh, you are young, you are free, you've at last got rid of parental authority; suddenly you get married, and authority is there again, and you don't have to report to your mother; you have to report to your wife."

Marriage, he suggested, requires adaptation. "It can be a regressive institution, and for all married couples it can be a traumatic experience. I think husbands, particularly when they are as busy as I was, are not as sensitive to that as they should be. Hopefully, we learn." However, he said, Margaret had not been completely unaware of the pressures of political life. "Don't overstate it," he said. "Her father had been a Cabinet Minister and she had been brought up as a little girl in politics." The Prime Minister suggested that her awareness of what politics could do to family life explained why "for a few years she remained completely outside it and didn't want to involve herself even in a simple political meeting until she had, I guess, assimilated that new status of not only a wife, but a wife of a prime minister." Explaining that sometimes she chose to accompany him on political occasions, as was the case during the 1974 election campaign, and sometimes she chose to stay at home, Trudeau said. "She'll make her choices and I'll respect them."

A couple of months later, Margaret, attending a Commonwealth Conference with her husband in Jamaica, declared to reporters that she could foresee the day when she would be out working and Trudeau would be staying at home to mind the house. Asked if the Prime Minister did much in the way of housework, she replied, "Yes, he does. He's a great help. I had no trouble with Pierre because he values freedom and he respects my freedom very much and he enjoys doing what he can to help. I don't demand too much of him because I have to be rational. He's a very busy man and I hope once, whenever that is, when politics is over in our life, we'll be able to share much more the responsibilities at home."

In February, 1977, Margaret was still maintaining that if Trudeau wanted to remain in politics for another four years, that would be fine with her. During an interview in Washington, she said that if Trudeau chose to remain for another term, "I would be very supportive of that. I want the decision to be based on his own personal feelings of whether he's fulfilling the task he set out to do, or whether he can do it." There was no point, she said, in "whining" but added, "Oh, I want my own house. Really, I think that would be very selfish and I think unfair because he would resent after awhile that I had talked him out of an important job."

In March, during Margaret's much-publicized trip to New York, the Prime Minister told a news conference that he did not expect his wife to alter her behavior, saying, "That's one of the prices you pay for being in politics." He was adamant about Margaret being free to do as she wished. "I'm sorry, but I don't expect Margaret to stop going to rock concerts and going to New York just because some people will be misled into thinking that she is not doing right. If other people judge it wrong and because of that don't like my anti-inflation program, too bad."

His shrewd answers almost succeeded in reducing Margaret's escapades to casual, everyday outings. Ignored was the question of the propriety of the Prime Minister's wife associating with people facing serious drug charges. Canada had come a long way since 1968, when Pierre Trudeau's lighthearted observation that there should be a chicken in every pot and some pot in every chicken, had aroused the wrath of anti-drug organizations.

"So a lady goes to a rock concert and then she goes to New York to visit a friend and to do some photography. . . . I don't think she can be blamed for disappointing the Canadian people or rocking the Canadian dollar. If that is how the media or people react, too bad, but I certainly wouldn't tell Margaret not to go or anything else."

Trudeau said that he and his wife had attended rock concerts together in the National Arts Centre in Ottawa—and drew chuckles from reporters by sticking a finger in his ear and grimacing. He said that in fact, the Stones weren't Margaret's favorite group; she preferred the Beatles. "But I hope she doesn't start seeing the Beatles."

His only comment about the propriety of Margaret's association with the Stones came after pointed questions from reporters. "I don't indulge in guilt by association, whether by commenting on that kind of question or putting two stories on the same page or beside each other."

In October, 1976, Trudeau consented to a long interview for a film profile being prepared by a French television network. During the interview, he explained his attitudes towards his wife, his upbringing and his children.

Q: "What quality do you admire most in a woman?"

A: "Grace."

Q: "Will you raise your children the same way you were raised?"

A: "I would like to avoid their enslavement to material things. It's marvelous to be able to appreciate a good meal, a good book, a great holiday. But I would consider it a kind of slavery if one were to suffer a sense of deprivation without these. And I hope that they will learn, as my parents taught me, a detachment from that sort of thing."

Q: "It seems that as a youngster you were unruly."

A: "Very boisterous, it seems. I never accepted authority to any great extent nor the argument of authority. I'm told that I always tried to have the last word with my father. That wasn't easy because he was a very spirited man. Later, I think it was true with my teachers and my colleagues. I am now discovering this in my children."

Q: "Which one of the three children has inherited most of these character traits?"

A: "Well, right now I see it mostly in the eldest, Justin, who always says, 'All right, but . . .'"

Q: "Why do you spend so much time with your children?"

A: "I find it marvelous. I have always been attracted by the transcendentalists, not the philosophers. Truth, beauty, that sort of thing delights me. And you find these things in a child, this creativity, this being which is forming and creating itself. I am enchanted by that."

Q: "Do you not see yourself reflected a bit (in your children)? Doesn't one try to find parts of oneself?"

A: "I have never been aware of that. I think I tried to make out in a way that one's children are better than oneself, (that they) do not repeat the mistakes one has made. And it seems that one doesn't succeed too well at this, but . . . yes, perhaps it is interesting to come upon a characteristic which reminds one of oneself, but that's not the main thing. Above all I see them as beings who are in the process of creating, forming themselves without modelling themselves on anyone."

Q: "I have seen you with your children for some days now. With them it is normal that they should have this sense of wonderment. But I find it also in you. Your enchantment with these small beings, your children, your sons, is obvious."

A: "I am very easily amazed by life. I don't think I'm discovering anything new. Whether it's something about a child or the first time I tasted tongue, I found it extraordinary . . . the first time I tried skindiving, the first time I tried parachuting . . . I always like to discover new sensations."

Q: "And the first time you met Margaret?"

A: "Oh, I remember that very well. It was in Tahiti. By some chance she was there with her parents and her sisters. And I found her eyes extraordinarily beautiful. And I still do."

Q: "You are very loving."

A: "I had forgotten her for a year or two, if I may say so, but I always remembered her eyes. And when I saw her again . . . Perhaps . . . No, it wasn't quite like that. I saw her again a few months later when I was campaigning for the Prime Ministership."

Q: "You knew that it was she?"

A: "No, to be truthful, not at that moment. I wasn't ready to say, 'That is the woman I shall marry in a year and a half,' but . . ."

Q: "How long was it before you knew?"

A: "Oh, I often have the impression that the woman knows before the man. As for me, I knew it a few months before my marriage. No, I knew it sooner than that. I knew that if I were going to marry anyone, it would be her, but I did not know whether I would get married at all."

Q: "Did you discuss it with her later? Did she know too?"

A: "Oh, yes. She pretends that she knew at least six months before I did."

Q: "Your marriage with Margaret isn't a traditional one. You are a feminist."

A: "I?"

Q: "Yes."

A: "If you like."

Q: "You have an arrangement, an agreement; I think you already said it isn't easy for her. She knew what she was letting herself in for. But the adjustment is difficult. She was a bit overshadowed. (After the marriage) there followed perhaps two or three different stages. She has really involved herself in the life of the wife of the Prime Minister. And then, she is always striving to have her own life, her own career. Each time she withdraws a bit in order to have a private lifestyle she ends up making headlines."

A: "Right. Yes, when she wears jeans to do her marketing and is spotted, she is photographed, although at that moment she would like to be alone and when she gets all dressed up to go to a reception, she is photographed. That's the game. No, I don't know whether I'm a feminist. But I have already said I believe that marriage is a regressive institution in the sense that one recreates the dependency relationship vis-a-vis one's parents . . . one's father if one is a girl and . . . one's mother if a boy. And it was a good thing that I did not marry sooner because I was very domineering and doubtless would have wanted to remake my wife—which is to say, destroy her personality. And it was only when I was able to accept that another person could be very different from myself, and that in spite of this I could love her, that I could make the gamble of getting married. But back to the point of view of the woman. Perhaps because of our institutions, society, the woman always remains a bit subjugated by marriage. Even Nature plays a part in this: it is she who produces the children; it is she who raises them, who looks after them more than the man. The male in this and preceding civilizations goes to work or to hunt and the woman is kept back, confined. I think that women are now beginning to leave this confinement, but it takes a great deal of maturity on their part—and on that of the man. There are people—you will know some—where the roles have changed, where the man looks after the children and the woman works. I find that . . . a lot of maturity is needed for that kind of thing. Unless that maturity is there, the marriage does not result in more freedom, but less."

Q: "She is very lovely, as everybody knows. It is obvious that you are very much in love . . . the whole world is aware of this. There is a certain tenderness between you as a couple. There is, however, an age difference between you and her which may (nevertheless) be comfortable for her. Is it comfortable for you? Because of her age, did she bring you a different outlook on life and things?"

A: "It is very comfortable for me because it allows me to skip a generation and to have with me someone from another generation who brings me a whole new outlook on things, even a different scale of values, not only for cultural and geographical reasons, because she comes from the west coast, but also because of her age within her generation. Here is a girl who was at university during the period of student unrest and dispute. Here is a girl who knew television in her childhood—which I didn't. There are all sorts of ways in which I find myself enriched by her and which attracted me to her. I don't know whether it's as easy for her. Certainly there are things she loves in me. But I think that she has suffered and continues to do so because she is not the mistress of a normal household, that she is in a sort of institution where people come and go and where she cannot, or only very rarely, cook. For that she has to go to the country. She has too many servants to be truly the mistress of her house. That is definitely very difficult for her. She fights it. And I encourage her in this, in making some other career for herself or finding other occupations. She has a lot of talent in the arts, for photography and she seems to be immersing herself more and more in these. I find it a good thing."

Q: "Speaking of cooking, has she sometimes cooked small meals for you?"

A: "Not small meals. Meals which took hours to prepare. That's one of the main things which attracted me to her. Even before we were married, she would come to the country to make a meal and did this with exquisite taste and when we are there on weekends, Saturday and Sunday, she makes very complicated dishes, or Japanese meals which take hours of preparation."

Q: "Japanese, that means finding the vegetables and. . ."

A: "Oh, yes, she goes to the market and finds all the most exotic things there. At bottom she is a very earthy woman. A sensual woman with both feet on the ground. A woman who wants to be a mother, a woman who also loves cooking, domestic things, and yet at the same time can go off into the clouds."

Q: "Sometimes she'll make a public statement. In your reaction, there is always the same admiration, you understand her completely."

A: "It's like the children, isn't it? I am always delighted to see what can emerge from a person whom one thinks one knows very well. Suddenly there is something new. In this sense, this is a woman I could never control, who will do whatever she pleases."

It is impossible for one to know what Pierre Trudeau actually felt when he and his wife drew up their public statement of separation. But certainly he was hurt, and certainly he will never be the same man in future that he once was when he first met gorgeous Margaret Sinclair on a small island on the other side of the earth.

15
Final Days?

Within a day or two of publication, it was impossible to obtain a copy of the issue of *People* magazine that contained the notorious interview with Margaret, in which she talked about her "strong sexual energies". Extra bundles of the magazine had been shipped to Canada, but advance publicity had sent readers rushing to the newsstands to snap up details of Margaret's latest escapades. Friends reported that Margaret was so nervous when she read the interview back in Ottawa that her hands were shaking. But later, according to other sources, she happily autographed copies of the magazine, and seemed pleased about her photographs.

Before leaving New York, she had told a reporter for the London *Daily Express*: "Don't condemn me as the Prime Minister's wife. Because I . . . I . . . I abdicate." But she denied the story when she was interviewed by the *New*

York Times. "How can the Prime Minister's wife abdicate? What I meant was that I was going to abdicate from attending a public engagement in Nova Scotia later this month." She said she would be "at Pierre's side when he needs me. I'm just going to be working with my photography, not shaking hands and smiling in crowded halls. I'm tired of that sort of thing." Trudeau said at his regular weekly press conference that Margaret was cancelling some of her engagements because she wanted some privacy. Then, referring to a dinner planned for March 12 in Ottawa, with British Prime Minister James Callaghan and his wife, Trudeau said, "I hope she doesn't cancel that one but that's a little down the line, but if she cancels in the weeks and months ahead, that's her right."

In the *Daily Express* interview, Margaret said: "I do not believe I'm going to be in Ottawa (on March 12). My plans are not to be in Ottawa. I'm not returning until Monday, so I'm afraid Pierre is going to be receiving Mr. Callaghan on his own, and doesn't want to." She said she felt "I'm in control. I feel like a spectator involved in something absurd and rather strange really. This has never happened to me before. I'm trying my best. I do love life and I do love people but sometimes, you know, when people start judging you on every small thing you do, it becomes difficult to be tolerant." Margaret returned to Ottawa on the day the Callaghan dinner was scheduled but did not attend. Later, she explained that her husband did not want her to be there.

At the end of March, a Toronto radio station broadcast a report that the Trudeaus were about to separate. The Prime Minister's Office quickly labelled the rumor "extremely unlikely". In Vancouver, Margaret's parents, who had expressed concern about their daughter's behavior, decided that the time had come to keep quiet. "We're not going to make any comments on anything you've heard," Mrs. Sinclair said. Her husband said the same thing. On April 7, Dan Turner, Margaret's long-time friend, told a television audience the Trudeaus had arranged a ninety-day separation "to find themselves some time to breathe." Turner, who works for the C.B.C., said on the network's Ottawa news program that the decision did not mean they were separating permanently. He said Margaret had told him about the arrangement.

The trial separation, Turner said, had begun before Margaret's visit to Toronto to see the Stones, and since then the Trudeaus had been avoiding each other. "A month ago I was so sure there was a breakup that I was going to write a story," Turner said. "Now, it seems less definite. It could go either way." Margaret was "in good shape. She's quite happy." There was "still a lot of affection . . . there will be a continuing relationship but they have not figured out what it will be."

Turner's observations seemed to have been borne out by the Prime Minister himself, who announced he was going on a ten-day skiing holiday—alone. "My wife will be staying with the children, to relieve these hard-worked maids," he said sarcastically at a news conference. Realizing that he was going to face questions about his marriage, Trudeau had attempted to forestall the reporters by making several inconsequential announcements and replying at length to questions on other subjects. "I can't quarrel with the concerns you might have on behalf of the public," Trudeau said, "but I think my marital status is my own business and that of my wife, thank you very much."

While Trudeau and Margaret both criticized reporters for their persistent questions, a *Washington Post* gossip columnist, Nancy Collins, reported that the aspiring photographer had showed remarkably similar vigor in her attempt to wrangle an interview with actress Elizabeth Taylor.

At the beginning of April, Margaret had traveled to Middleburg, Virginia, trying to take pictures of Miss Taylor and John Warner, her latest husband, the columnist said. Margaret called the Warner farm several times asking to see Miss Taylor. "Liz told her she'd love to have her for tea, but no pix." Later, the columnist reported, Margaret had cornered Miss Taylor in a Middleburg gas station. "But alas, our Maggie retreated." According to the columnist, "Liz found it all very odd indeed, especially when she found that Maggie had called John while she was out. John met Maggie for a drink in Middleburg's Cock and Bull (a tavern) after the church service he attended alone. Ever persevering, our heroine tried to talk John into the story, but failed." Margaret had met the Warners in February, when she accompanied the Prime Minister to a dinner given by the Canadian ambassador in Washington.

Evidence that the Trudeaus' marriage was on the rocks continued to accumulate. At Easter, Margaret attended an Anglican church service in Ottawa, although she had converted to Catholicism when she had married and had raised her three children as Catholics. An acquaintance interpreted the gesture as "Margaret's way of saying the marriage was over. It was an extremely blatant statement of her feelings." In addition, reporters noticed that neither Margaret nor the Prime Minister were wearing their wedding rings. Finally, there was the incident of the black eye. Margaret showed at least eight reporters in Ottawa her blackened right eye and told them her husband had beaten her in an angry battle over her conduct in New York. However, others swore she had returned from New York with the shiner; a third version had it that Margaret had used makeup to fake the injury.

After the separation, Margaret told an American television audience that she had made the decision to live her own life when she learned that her friend, Queen Alia of Jordan, had been killed in a helicopter crash on February 9. "She was my age, with three small children and it made me realize that for the first time . . . that you can't put off forever what you want to do because there may not be a tomorrow." She said it moved her deeply to realize that Queen Alia "doesn't live anymore, and I sort of felt I must live myself, I must live my own life." She said Queen Alia had encouraged her to make the personal sacrifices that go with the job of being a Prime Minister's wife. "We had a common sort of bond together. She knew I was sort of suffering in my own way and encouraged me to sacrifice a lot and encouraged me to give up my personal dreams to help my husband and to further his work. And then one day she was killed. . . . I was broken-hearted on a personal level, but it also moved me deeply to understand that someone who had everything going for her—a beautiful, beautiful person, beautiful children and a very good relationship with her husband— doesn't live anymore."

Considering the startling similarities between Margaret and Queen Alia, it was not at all surprising that close bonds had developed. Nor was it surprising that after her separation, Margaret dined several times in New York with the former playboy, King Hussein. Queen Alia, who had been tall, blonde, and, like Margaret, crazy about bluejeans, had married the King in 1972, a year after the Trudeaus' headline-making wedding in Vancouver. Before her marriage, she had been simply Alia Toukan, daughter of Baha-Eddi Toukan, a former Jordanian ambassador to the United Nations. While Margaret had developed an instant crush on Trudeau upon first meeting him during a south seas island vacation in 1967,

Queen Alia had nurtured a secret love for King Hussein for years before they were married.

The King was a friend of her family, and would visit with them whenever he was traveling through countries where her diplomat father was posted. But Hussein, who had ascended to the Jordanian throne at the age of eighteen, was already married when he visited Alia's family. In fact he had been married twice—first to Egyptian Dina Abdel Hamid and then to an English-woman, Tony Avril Gardiner. He had divorced them both. Knowing he was married at that time, Alia had kept her love a secret. The King began dating her only after divorcing his second wife.

Although she was born in Jordan, Alia's style was very much that of a North-American woman. She shared Margaret's fondness for rock music and had been educated at Hunter College in New York City, where, like Margaret, she had studied social psychology and political science. Margaret may well have been inspired by the young Queen, who spoke out courageously for women's rights in Jordan, where the Moslem religion had made women subservient for centuries. In a country where most women remained very much in the background, having babies and keeping house, Queen Alia, with the encouragement of her husband, had tackled male-dominated fields and thrived. Knowing that she ran the risk of exciting gossip among the King's subjects, she had nevertheless gained a daredevil reputation by racing around on motorcycles and flying about in helicopters.

Before her marriage, she had worked for the Royal Jordanian Airlines as a public-relations representative, where she had mingled on equal terms with the wealthy, the powerful and the influential in Jordan—government officials, visiting diplomats, and important journalists. Naturally, she had been reluctant to give it all up after her marriage.

Like Margaret, Queen Alia had had an impulsive spirit. She had been on her way to inspect a hospital in mountains 200 miles south of Jordan's capital when she was killed. Had it not been for her impulsiveness, she might have been alive today, for the visit to the hospital had been a spur-of-the-moment decision, made only hours before she left. Had the Queen lived, perhaps she could have continued to exert a positive effect upon Margaret. But it was not meant to be.

Once Margaret had begun her "ultimate freedom trip" to Toronto and New York, she did not return to live at 24 Sussex again. Despite that, she still talks positively about the future. She says of her children: "I talk regularly with them on the telephone, and as well I supervise very carefully the way the girls who are helping raise the children—the attitudes they have, their diets. I feel that I'm absolutely in control of their lives. I don't think women really have to spend twenty-four hours a day with their children in order to be a good mother. We have a very intense, good relationship." Pierre Trudeau, she still maintains, "is an excellent father. It's silly for me to even think of having three small children with me in

New York, living the kind of life that I'll be living and working hard. There is absolutely no question that they will stay with Pierre and stay in the home where they have been born and raised."

And the future?

"Oh, we haven't settled anything. Pierre and I have decided not to live together, but we have totally agreed that we're still going to be together, the parents of our children, and I think we're going to have a very happy relationship with the family."

Will Pierre and Margaret remain together?; will they be reunited? Only time, really, will tell . . . as it has told so much in the past. It will, undoubtedly, be interesting to see what happens in the future life of Margaret Trudeau. With a past as complex and mystifying as hers, anything, really, is possible. Perhaps she and Pierre will get back together again for a time, perhaps permanently; perhaps they will remain friends. It is even conceivable that they could end up bitter enemies.

But no matter what the future has in store for her, or them, Margaret will remain an interesting enigma for Canadians for some time to come. No one will easily forget the winsome girl who won the heart of the Prime Minister and captured the love of an entire country.

SOME IMPORTANT DATES
IN THE LIFE OF
MARGARET TRUDEAU

September 10, 1948: Margaret Joan Sinclair born in Vancouver

March 4, 1971: Margaret Sinclair marries Pierre Elliott Trudeau

December 25, 1971: Justin Pierre James Trudeau born

December 25, 1973: Alexandre Emmanuel Trudeau born

September, 1974: Margaret spends two weeks in hospital for emotional stress

October 2, 1975: Michel Charles-Emile Trudeau born

January, 1976: Trip to Latin America

March, 1977: Margaret departs for "ultimate freedom trip"

May 27, 1977: Formal announcement of separation from Pierre